Fundraising Without Fundraisers

A Nonprofit Step-by-Step Guide to Generating Revenue Using Untraditional Methods

Pam Hogan

Community Press

ISBN: 978-0-9794294-8-4
Community Press
Box 31667
San Francisco, CA 94131
Orders@ACommunityPress.com

San Francisco, California

Contents

Introduction

The problem is an old one. It's one that you and anyone who has spent any time at all in the social sector understands all too well. There is never enough money to do all of the things you would like or need to do, and the search for funding never ends. It's the nature of the beast. But, the fact that you've invested in this material demonstrates that you are interested in discovering new ways of acquiring funds that step outside of traditional means.

Let me assure you from the outset that this book does not discuss one strategy that uses the business as usual approach to raising funds, and, as the title suggests, it certainly doesn't discuss fundraisers. What you will discover are multiple strategies for generating unrestricted no strings attached sustainable income that will flow into your organization.

Allow me first to take a minute to provide you with a little bit of my story. Sometimes it feels like I was born to serve. Since I can remember, I've been associated with one service-based organization or another. I've worked for nonprofits, volunteered for them, written, produced and given trainings for them. I have earned a master's degree in nonprofit administration, and I've provided hundreds of consulting and training hours to thousands of staff members, and clients alike, in the social sector across the country. And, through the years I've seen firsthand the toll it takes trying to come up with programs that are tethered to new funding, hoping your base will rally and give more than the previous year, and facing the fear that if current funding gets cut there will be serious repercussions.

Fortunately, with a shift in thinking about funding there are other ways to acquire revenue. This book is intended to be a catalyst for that shift. It will describe strategies for creating a sustainable revenue stream that you can benefit from year after year and expand upon as you choose.

If I may, please allow me to make one request. If you feel any resistance, please make an effort to push through it and stay with me to the end. If you start to hear yourself saying, "oh, we could never pull that off" or, "well, she lost me there," just make a mental note but keep moving. You owe it to yourself to get everything this book has to offer, and you won't get that if you put it down without completing it.

The Problem and Its Solution

It's no secret that traditionally when individuals are asked to support an organization it's done with an appeal to their altruism. They're asked to give to your cause because according to you it's a good cause, "We're trying to end hunger, this is a worthy cause, won't you help us achieve our mission through your financial support?" This is the altruistic paradigm that has been in place for years.

However, the problem with an altruism-centered approach is that it limits you in the following ways: (1) you will only get money from people who know what you do, or those who have the time and desire to learn about what you do, and then feel moved to support what you do; (2) you are limited to people who are oriented toward donating to charity; (3) you are limited to people who will hand over money without receiving anything tangible in return. Clearly when asking for straight donations you limit yourself.

What would happen if instead of depending on altruism, with its limitations, you gave people another reason to support you, a selfish reason, a reason that's benefit-centered? You would expand your reach exponentially. When you can answer the question, "what's in it for me?" with a tangible benefit you can reach far more people with far fewer limitations.

The truth is, we may not all be philanthropists, but we are consumers. We don't have to be convinced that satisfying a desire is a good idea, it's what we do. This means you have a wonderful opportunity to marry the public's affinity toward nonprofits with the public's habit of satisfying their desires. When you address people as the consumers that they are, rather than the philanthropists that you want them to be everything changes. This is the reason a shift in thinking is so important.

A great example of this shift can be seen in eco-conscious green marketing. Somewhere along the line they made a clear and deliberate shift from a *what's in it for the environment* message to a *what's in it for me* message. Eco-friendly products at one time were described as being good for the *planet*, then the focus shifted to them being good for *you.* They were safer for you, they were cheaper for you. The focus also shifted to direct benefits—your health, superior performance, good taste, convenience. Why did they make these major shifts? Because with the first approach of *what's in it for the planet* they were primarily targeting an eco-conscious group of consumers, and that group wasn't large enough to sustain them. But with nothing more than a shift to a *what's in it for me* message they expanded their reach significantly.

Addressing the consumer in us all is a strategy that the Girl Scouts of the USA has utilized for decades. It's doubtful that most people could tell you the mission of the Girl Scouts, but they could probably name their favorite Girl Scouts cookie. Through the sale of their cookies, the Girl Scouts receives funds from people who were never scouts, people who don't know the organization's mission, and people who don't even have kids. They do this by tapping into our desire for a tasty snack. A snack that we justify buying because we tell ourselves that these cookies help out a good cause as well as being tasty.

However, if the Girl Scouts didn't have cookies and they just called you on the telephone and solicited you for a straight donation, then you would no doubt want to know what mission your money was supporting. Here is their mission: *Girl Scouting builds girls of courage, confidence, and character, who make the world a better place.* When asking for straight donations in support of that mission, they are suddenly competing against a lot of other organizations, for example, Girls Inc. Here's their mission: *Girls Incorporated is dedicated to inspiring all girls to be strong, smart, and bold.* So now you have this person from the Girl Scouts on the phone asking for a straight donation in support of courage, confidence, and character, and you have to ask yourself if that's better than strong, smart, and bold. But with cookies in hand, there's no need for questions. The Girls Scouts has done a great job of marrying altruism and consumerism, they sell 200 million boxes of cookies a year. At about $4 a box, it looks like the marriage has paid off nicely. And I'm going to show you how it can pay off for you as well.

As we begin to discuss income, I feel it's important to have a conversation about profits. Over the years, I've entered into conversations with some directors who actually believed that nonprofits were not allowed to earn a profit, which makes it important to take a moment to discuss this. Nonprofits are allowed, and do, in fact, earn a profit. What nonprofits cannot do is allow those profits to inure to the benefit of a private shareholder or individual. Whereas private sector companies often tie bonuses or salaries to net profits, a nonprofit cannot.

It makes sense to also take this time to discuss UBIT, Unrelated Business Income Tax. Income generated from some of the strategies we will be discussing might be categorized as unrelated business income. Why is that? Because the IRS says, "if an exempt organization regularly carries on a trade or business that is not substantially related to its exempt purpose, the organization is subject to tax on its income from that unrelated trade or business." That tax is at the regular corporate rate. A nonprofit may earn money from unrelated business income. They may, in fact, earn a great deal of money from an unrelated business income. Look at National Geographic, a documented figure I still have on hand from 1982 reports them as earning $22 million in taxable advertising revenue that year, in addition to that year's

$152 million untaxable subscription and membership revenues. Yes, nonprofits may earn a profit, they just cannot line their pockets with those profits. And, nonprofits may also earn taxable revenue, they just need to understand what the IRS wants to see in this regard.

The IRS is concerned with two things when it comes to taxable revenue: (1) they want the amount of time you expend in that undertaking to be minimal in comparison with your other undertakings, and (2) they want the undertaking to relate to your exempt purpose. A conversation with your tax accountant should help you see how you can join the organizations that have learned how to marry consumerism and altruism using the strategies you are about to learn.

The forerunners are certainly out there. Goodwill sells goods through their thrift stores. The Museum of Natural History publishes magazines. Cultural and environmental organizations publish calendars and books. Some organizations own parking lots, some own vending machines. Some earn money through the sale, lease, and rental of land and buildings. This book is going to show you how you can generate revenue through untraditional methods as well.

You are about to gain access to 16 strategies for generating an income stream of $50,000, $100,000 or more per year. When you implement several strategies, the sky's the limit on the income you can generate for your organization. Now, just because we're talking substantial income doesn't mean we're talking complex strategies. To follow are feasible simple to execute strategies; which is why it's possible to finish this book on Friday and start implementing on Monday, regardless of the size of your staff or budget.

Lay Out

So let me tell you how I've laid this book out for you. Section One contains *The What.* It will provide an introduction to all 16 strategies. This is the place where brainstorming is encouraged.

Section Two is where the meat is, it covers *The How.* I walk you step-by-step through the launching of each strategy in this section.

Once you know what and how, we'll have a conversation about *Strategic Financing.* And, we finish with an *Implementation Plan* that will serve as a road map for moving forward. So, let's get started.

The What

STRATEGY NUMBER 1: Tie Into Movies and Documentaries Aligned with Your Cause

In 1993, Tom Hanks and Denzel Washington brought mainstream attention to AIDS in the movie *Philadelphia.* Three years earlier, *Awakenings* drew attention to Parkinson Disease. In 2007, *The Pursuit of Happyness* showed how easy it is for someone trying so hard to still become homeless. And in 2009, *Precious* horrified us with an up-close look at abuse and inner city life. From medical conditions to social causes, the movie titles are familiar.

In spite of being fictitious, movies stimulate conversation and they get people thinking; in short, they do what you do, they raise awareness. Documentaries, naturally, do the same thing. When the subject of movies and documentaries align with your cause, it makes sense for your organization to take advantage of their power by offering these films to the public.

The documentary *D Tour,* for example, follows Pat Spurgeon, a member of a band who has a failing kidney. The film chronicles all of the challenges associated with being on tour, self-administering dialysis, while waiting and hoping for a kidney transplant. An organization associated with kidney disease, diabetes, or organ donation could sell that film for years. Just as an organization focused on the environment might still be selling copies of the 2006 documentary *Who Killed the Electric Car.*

Documentaries, whether blockbuster hits or obscure titles, retain their relevancy long after their release date, allowing you to generate income from them for years. A documentary whose topic is aligned with your cause is a gift that has been handed to you on a silver platter. In the next section, I'll tell you exactly how to find and purchase such DVDs at a wholesale price, and I'll show you how easy it is to market them, but for now, take a minute to jot down any documentaries or movies you're aware of that align with your mission.

STRATEGY NUMBER 2: Tie Into Books That Forward Your Mission

Whether you know it or not, your organization is a better place to sell books than bookstores. Books compete with each other for attention on bookstore shelves, and many never see the light of day. In fact, the majority of books sent to bookstores are returned to their publisher, which is why smart book marketers also use other outlets to reach the group of people for whom the book was written. After all, it makes sense that a book on buying your first fishing boat, for example, would sell better at a store that sells fishing gear than at a store that sells books. You reach a certain group of people. You too can be an outlet that gets books into the hands of the people for whom they were intended. Find the books written for your people, and you can very easily generate an income stream from their sale.

The beauty of books is that, like documentaries, their value extends well beyond their copyright date. I can't think of a better example of that than *The Catcher in the Rye*. Published in 1951, this book still sells 250,000 copies a year!

Beyond the books already in print, there are 190,000 nonfiction books published each and every year in the United States. These are titles written for no other reason than to educate people about a topic—a topic that just might be aligned with your cause. And, there's no shortage of options when it comes to fiction either. A new book of fiction is published every 30 minutes.

With such a large number of books being published year after year, it's doubtful that there aren't a few titles out there that tie into your cause in one way or another, whether nonfiction or fiction. But, if your cause is so obscure that you can't find a book that ties in with it, there are always books that inspire, books like *The Tao of Daily Living,* and the *Chicken Soup for the Soul* series. There are over 100 topics in this series on every subject imaginable. There's a *Chicken Soup for the Soul* for teens, pre-teens, parents, dieters, prisoners, brides, golfers, travelers, dog lovers, cat lovers, survivors of economic crises and cancer. You name it, and Jack Canfield and Mark Victor Hansen have collected inspirational stories on the topic. There are books being published and there are films and documentaries being produced on a regular basis that will either educate, entertain, or inspire your people, allowing you to generate an income stream in the process.

STRATEGY NUMBER 3: Personalize Merchandise with Messages Aligned with Your Cause

You only need to walk down the street, or go into an office or a home to see that the idea of personalized merchandise is one that Americans have embraced wholeheartedly. When a message resonates with us we want to put it on our cars, wear it on our chests, and stick it on our refrigerators. We like our mugs to cheer us up and our calendars to motivate us. Messages and message boards abound. As an organization that exists to spread a message, you have an opportunity to benefit from this phenomenon.

Let's take as an example an organization in the Bay Area that educates sufferers and doctors alike about lymphedema, a condition that manifests itself after ones lymphatic system has been damaged, for example, when lymph nodes are removed during cancer surgeries. This organization's biggest hurdle is the fact that even many doctors don't know what to tell their patients about this unnatural swelling that occurs in an arm or a leg affected by the condition. In fact, the condition is often triggered by medical professionals taking a patient's blood pressure, or drawing blood from the affected side. So, education and awareness are key, so as to prevent triggering the condition's initial onset. Imagine the messages this organization could print on merchandise: *Ask Your Doctor Before It's Too Late* or *What Your Doctor Doesn't Know Could Hurt You*, are just a couple that come to mind. By not inserting the word lymphedema, the organization allows these messages to resonate with the public on various personal levels.

The messages you can create are only limited by your imagination, and there are countless items to then print those messages on. The next section will walk you through all of the steps for executing this strategy.

What message could you imagine having printed on an item?

STRATEGY NUMBER 4: Compile a CD or DVD of Compelling Stories

We've been enthralled by stories since we were children. And, as adults we've all been captivated, at some time or another, by a real-world story. Advertising campaigns use stories because of the way they tap into our emotions. Teachers use stories to drive home a point in a way that only stories can. Public speakers use stories to hold an audience's attention. Kathy Levine, formerly one of the top salespeople at the multimedia retailer QVC, is quoted as saying that, "selling is a matter of capturing people's attention and holding it with a good story." What can we say, people like stories. So, give them one.

Let them hear the compelling stories from the mouths of the young people you help, the seniors you assist, whatever group you serve. Stories allow us to bond with your mission on an emotional level. They can help you bring awareness to what your organization does in a way that's unique to storytelling. By creating a CD or DVD of these compelling stories, you accomplish all of these things, while generating income for your organization.

If you want to hear an excellent example of how fascinating simple stories told by average people can be, check out NPR's *This American Life* with Ira Glass. Recordings of the show can be found at thisamericanlife.org.

If you have a story that is best captured visually, capture it on video. It's funny how we'll create brochures, and we'll write letters, and we'll make websites all designed to draw people to our message, but when someone says use a DVD for the same purpose we freeze. We get sucked into believing it will cost tens of thousands of dollars, or we get stopped by some other internal roadblock. Ignore all of that noise, resistance, and fear and believe me when I say that we're not talking about a Hollywood production here. This strategy is about capturing the message economically. I'll be going into great detail on how to do that in the next section. But, the great thing about CDs and DVDs is that they command a nice price in the marketplace, while the cost for duplication is very inexpensive, leaving you with a healthy profit margin.

So far, we've covered films that raise awareness about your cause, books that forward your mission, personalized products that convey a message aligned with your cause, CDs or DVDs that relate compelling stories. With these four strategies alone, you have quite the makings of an online store here, a store that will work for you 24 hours a day, seven days a week.

Why not give some thought to the kinds of stories you could capture, either through video or audio, understanding that brainstorming doesn't mean commitment, and see what jumps out at you.

STRATEGY NUMBER 5: Offer Support Products That Serve the Needs of Your Stakeholders

Here is a question that deserves serious consideration: What items do your people leave your office, website, or phone call to go buy from someone else? These are your stakeholders. What needs of theirs are you neglecting or ignoring? When you give some serious thought to these questions, you'll see why providing support products makes a great deal of sense.

There's no reason for your people to see you as the place where they get everything for free, while they see other organizations as the place where they pay for everything, when they would be willing to hand the money over to you just as easily.

Consider an organization whose mission is centered around serving people who have diabetes, couldn't they sell blood sugar level testers? What about the organization that provides education on avoiding a stroke? They give Mrs. Jones brochures that recommend she monitor her blood pressure regularly, so why couldn't they help her follow that recommendation by making it easy to buy a blood pressure monitor? An organization focused on the environment could sell eco-friendly products they have researched to be the most effective at what they do.

If you think broadly about the needs of your stakeholders, you should have no trouble forming a list of support products that will help you better serve your people and generate income at the same time.

When you fail to offer such support products, you force your people to put in the time and effort required to research where they can find the products they need. Ironically, you may even be providing them with referrals for places they can buy the products, rather than simply selling them yourself. This is income that you could easily generate, while doing a better job of serving your people's needs.

Never stop asking yourself, "what are we making our stakeholders leave our office, our phone conversation, our website to go buy from someone else?"

In the next section, I'm going to show you how to find wholesale suppliers of any item imaginable, but for now why not have a brainstorming session where you jot down whatever support products come to mind. Don't reject any idea, just brainstorm without judgment.

STRATEGY NUMBER 6: Produce Special Reports

When you're in need of information in a hurry, special reports can really be a life saver. Whether you've run into trouble taking your carburetor apart, or you can't figure out the table setting for a dinner party you're throwing, special reports offer specialized information that people value and are willing to pay for. Delivered digitally as a PDF, a person can download the material within seconds of entering their credit card information.

Special reports have a price range that extends from $3 on up into the hundreds. The majority of them are on the short side. Some reports selling for $10 and $15 are only five pages long.

Rather than write a book on a topic, it's become very common to write a few special reports instead. After all, that 18 chapter book may sell for $29.95, but if you can take that same information and produce 18 special reports that sell for $10 each, you have the potential of earning $180 instead. Same information—much different price tag.

Producing special reports would allow you to give the kind of attention to a topic that a phone call or a brochure, or even a website isn't always capable of. In the middle of the night, a person looking for real and immediate answers can purchase a special report and get the comprehensive information they need.

The beauty of digital products, like special reports, is that they allow you to get paid over and over again without having to be replenished. Long after you've retired, the agency will still be benefiting from special reports you've put into the marketplace.

In the next section, you'll see exactly how easy it is to create special reports. In fact, I bet you already have the makings of several in your possession. In no time at all, you can have hundreds of dollars worth of reports out there generating revenue for you. And, if you prefer, you don't even have to do the writing yourself. I'll walk you through all of the steps for this income generator, and show you examples of reports in the marketplace in the next section.

Why not take a minute to sketch out some topics you could see being turned into a special report. Don't think about writing it, you're not committing to doing that, just sketch out some topics.

STRATEGY NUMBER 7: Produce eBooks

Just like special reports, electronic books are also downloadable material that provide information-hungry buyers with immediate access to information they need. And, just like special reports, as a digital product eBooks require no printing or replenishing of inventory.

The price for eBooks vary depending on their length and how specialized the material. Don't be confused by the price tags you find for Amazon's eBooks sold for their Kindle e-reader. It's no secret that Amazon's aim has always been to sell their Kindle, while making lots of low-cost material available for it. This is evidenced by their royalty structure. Authors receive 70 percent of the retail price of eBooks priced at $9.99 and lower, and only 35 percent on books priced higher than that.

Long before there were eBook readers, however, buyers of eBooks were downloading PDFs, and that trend continues. You'll find 50 page PDF eBooks selling for $17, with longer ones selling for $47, $77, $97, and into the hundreds for more specialized topics. In the next section, I'll give you some specific examples of the revenue being generated from the sale of eBooks.

STRATEGY NUMBER 8: Produce Instructional CDs or DVDs

We can't deny the fact that we not only live in the Information Age, but that we live in a time where that information is expected to meet people where they are, for the type of learners that they are, for the type of schedules that they have. How many different ways are you reaching your people? Is it through your website and other printed material? America has 30 million adults who are unable to read the printed word, how are you reaching them? It's time to start meeting people where they are.

If you have information to impart, you have to start thinking of the many ways people want to consume that information, and provide it for them in that format. People take home study courses, they listen to audio programs, and they invest in training DVDs. Look at all of the instructional material you can buy these days on CD, Mp3, or DVD. Want to lose that weight? Pop in this DVD and learn from a personal trainer. Want to learn a new language? Listen to these language CDs. Don't have time to read but have tons of commute hours? Pick up an audio book. The private sector gets it, and it's time for the social sector to get it too.

You know better than most the educational needs of your stakeholders, this is your chance to address them. If the only thing holding you back from meeting those needs is the belief that it's too complicated or it's cost prohibitive to produce an instructional program, put those thoughts aside. Producing an instructional CD or DVD is not as complex or as costly as one might think.

For now, simply give some thought to what you find yourself frequently explaining over the phone or in emails. Think about the topics other agencies call on you for. Consider the trainings you currently provide.

Take a minute to consider what educators, the general public, business owners, prisoners, government agencies, or HR managers would be better off having learned from you. Give some thought to the answer to these questions. They could be telling you what CD or DVD the marketplace needs from you.

STRATEGY NUMBER 9: Host a Contest

Contests have been around for years, and with good reason. They're fun for participants who part with a nominal fee to enter, and they're a great income generator for the host. Although you'll find contests these days with no fees, often judged by the public on social networking sites, these kinds of contests are really more marketing buzz than anything. And, they aren't the kinds of contests we're talking about here. We're talking about the real deal, with entry fees that allow you to generate a nice income stream, with a select group of judges that critically examine entries, with awards and recognition. We're talking about something that you can be proud to hold year after year, and for which you can develop a following. As the host, a contest will raise awareness about your cause and organization in addition to raising funds.

Hosting a contest might sound like a big undertaking, but it really isn't very different from hosting a fundraiser dinner. Both involve charging a fee for entrance and engaging people in a pleasurable experience. Fundraiser dinners, however, tend to be mired in fixed costs that can cause them to be more risky than a contest.

It's not as if this is uncharted territory for the social sector. The San Diego Natural History Museum regularly hosts a Best of Nature Photo Contest, and St. Francis of Assisi Catholic Church has become known for its BBQ cooking contest, just to name a couple.

Contest entry fees vary. St. Francis of Assisi charges $250 to participate in their BBQ cooking contest. Poetry and photo contests are on the lower end of the scale. They run $5, $10 and $25 per poem or photo entered. The fees go up from there. You'll find entry fees of $30 for songwriting contests, $50 for screenwriting, and it varies with books, but $75 is not uncommon. And these prices are for meeting the first deadline, the price typically increases as the cutoff approaches.

Contests tend to pick up momentum over time, with the number of participants growing. After 10 years of holding a contest for written works, the group *Independent Publisher* now has over 1,500 participants from all 50 states, eight Canadian provinces, and 16 other countries from around the world. They charge $75 per title before a certain date, then the fee rises to $85 for about two months, leveling off at $95 for the last two months before the cut-off. Now, assuming one entry per publisher, which is hard to imagine, and further assuming everyone submits with the early-bird price, which is also hard to imagine, but just doing the math of 1,500 participants submitting one title at $75 a pop, there's $112,500 on the table.

Contests have incredible income potential, and they're an extremely fun way for the public to express themselves on a subject that resonates with your organization. The day nonprofits conjure the image of a fun creative contest rather than a fundraiser dinner is going to be a great day.

STRATEGY NUMBER 10: Host Webinars and Teleseminars

Webinars and teleseminars allow people from all across the globe to attend the same class without anyone having to leave home.

A teleseminar allows participants to dial a number at a designated time, enter a code, and join a call. From a technical standpoint, callers connect using a telephone bridge line, which is basically a lower quality less costly conference call. On a webinar, participants enable software that allows them to view your computer screen in addition to hearing you.

In the social sector, you may primarily find teleseminars and webinars offered for free, but in the private sector they can cost anywhere from $29.95 to $199 for a 60 or 90 minute session.

There are many ways to generate revenue with webinars or teleseminars. We will discuss them all in the next section.

STRATEGY NUMBER 11: Hold Workshops

Every day of the week, individuals attend a professional or personal development workshop of some kind. There are trainers who earn a good living holding these workshops, and your organization just might have the makings of a workshop topic that will allow you to do the same.

Maybe you've thought of holding workshops before and you talked yourself out of it, for one reason or another. Well, in the next section I'm going to explore the many ways you can successfully apply this strategy. Workshops can be extremely profitable. With only 25 participants paying $797 to attend, you would generate over $19,000 each workshop. If you only held six workshops a year, you would raise over $119,000.

Why not take this time to do a little brainstorming around topics for teleseminars, webinars, and workshops. Don't worry about who might do the training, or any of the nuts and bolts, we'll discuss those details in the next section. But for now, why not take the time to consider some topics before you move on.

STRATEGY NUMBER 12: Monetize Services You Currently Offer For Free

You may dislike the idea of charging people for services or products you currently offer for free, but it deserves a conversation.

This strategy doesn't necessarily involve charging all of your users, or charging for all of your services, or charging individuals who are of low income. But, it does involve looking at your price structure, and at the services or products you currently provide, and thinking about who benefits from them, and then examining your options.

Maybe you've already given some thought to what this might entail. The question is what's been holding you back? Things go up, social services included. If monetizing some of your services allows your organization to remain viable, it deserves consideration. Having you around is far more important than having all of your resources provided at no cost.

In the next section, I'll provide a few twists to this topic, and talk about some creative ways for monetizing current offerings.

STRATEGY NUMBER 13: Promote Affiliate Products

What do Barnes and Noble, Dell Computer, Discover Card, and Amazon have in common? They all offer an affiliate program.

Affiliate marketing allows you to earn a commission every time someone clicks on a website link that has been assigned to you and takes a certain action. Let's say an organization recommends some useful books or products to its stakeholders, providing links to those items from their website. If the organization had simply signed up to be an affiliate for those products, they would earn a commission every time someone clicked on those links and made a purchase.

A few months ago I bought a $47 eBook. The affiliate for that product earned $21 as a result of my purchase. What did he do to earn that commission? He simply sent me an email about the eBook because he thought I'd be interested in it, which clearly I was. When I clicked on his unique affiliate link inside of the email, it made it possible for him to earn his commission.

The beauty of affiliate marketing is that you simply promote a service or product you would normally recommend; you then play no further role in the transaction.

In the case of the $47 eBook I purchased, the young man's $21 earnings were a one-time commission. But, what if instead of a product it was a service that had a monthly fee? Well, then that $21 would be earned each and every month.

Marketing affiliate products or services requires very light lifting, yet it can generate substantial income. It will be broken down to its most basic parts in the next section.

STRATEGY NUMBER 14: Offer a Coaching Program

Coaching offers you the chance to enhance and expand your range of services, while providing individuals with intimate access to your expertise on a subject. When you think about it, nonprofits and coaches have a few things in common. They both serve a niche, they both address the challenges their clients contend with, and people value the expertise and resources of both. The common ground is apparent. In fact, some of what you already do might be categorized as coaching.

You don't have to be the world's most renowned expert on a topic to be a coach. Think of professional athletes, not only do they continue to use coaches after they have proven themselves to be one of the best in the game, but in many cases, they use a coach who never had the same level of success in the field. Why is that? It's because being a good coach doesn't require that you are the best in the field. Well-rounded knowledge on the subject, a fresh eye, and a better vantage point from which to assess a situation is what people need most in a coach.

Coaches aren't limited to sports by any means. There's a coaching program on every topic imaginable—one Google search confirms that. There could be a coaching program that makes sense for your organization to offer as well.

People pay as little as $1,200 a year to $100,000 a year for coaching programs. Now, just in case you envision coaching as being very time consuming because you're thinking of a one-on-one model, you'll be pleased to know that the coaching model discussed in the next section is not very labor intensive at all.

If you serve clients who are of low income, fight back any resistance you may be experiencing over this strategy. The discussion in the next section on potential workshop clients encompasses this scenario.

STRATEGY NUMBER 15: Offer Language Classes

Does your organization serve individuals whose first language is not English? Does your community demonstrate an interest in learning how to speak a second language? What about your community college, does it offer foreign language classes? If you answered *yes* to any of these questions, there may be an opportunity for you to generate revenue filling a need in the community by hiring a professional to teach small group language classes.

Many adults who want to learn a new language look beyond community college because classes tend to be crowded, it can mean more of a commitment than some people have time for, and the academic approach used for teaching a foreign language doesn't appeal to everyone. These individuals tend to turn to small group language classes. You can become a resource for these individuals by offering such classes.

While serving your community, you can generate revenue that is extremely scalable. I'll walk you through all of the numbers in the next section.

STRATEGY NUMBER 16: Host a Membership Site

Membership sites are websites specifically designed to address the concerns, needs and interests of its paying members. To appreciate the power of a membership site, imagine a person with a condition, a circumstance, or a lifestyle that's not widely experienced or understood in search of information and community. A membership site offers this individual exactly that, access to fresh pertinent information, and a community to interact with.

Membership sites span a wide range of topics, some are more lighthearted than others. There are sites for golfers, tennis players, pet owners, and divorced women. There are membership sites that cater to Internet marketers, speakers, accountants, restaurant owners, and nurses. There are sites designed to help its members lose weight, trade stocks, train their dogs, and write their first book.

In the next section, you'll get a link to a site that will show you several membership sites where people are paying $9.99 a month to hundreds of dollars per month for membership.

If you acquire only one new member a day, paying $19.95 a month, at the end of the year you would have generated over $87,000. This is revenue that continues to come into the organization year after year, expanding with your membership base.

Think about the people you serve, or a subset of those people, or the people who also serve this population who might benefit from a site that caters to their needs. We'll discuss a wide range of possibilities when we tease this strategy out in the next section.

The How

STRATEGY NUMBER 1: Tie Into Movies and Documentaries Aligned with Your Cause

Beginning back at the top of our strategy list, let's jump right into the steps for selling movies and documentaries. To sell DVDs, obviously, you first have to find those that align with your organization's cause. Two sites that make this very easy are amazon.com and rottentomatoes.com. At Amazon's site, you just need to select *Movies and TV* from the pull-down menu, and type into the search box a term associated with your cause.

You would do the same thing to find documentaries, but in addition to your term you must also type *Documentaries on DVD* into the search box. For example, while in the *Movies and TV* category you might type *homelessness, Documentaries on DVD* to see all of the documentaries Amazon has for sale on the subject. By visiting Amazon's site, you will also get a sense of retail prices. With a title in mind, you can visit rottentomatoes.com and view a trailer of it, and see what score audiences have given it.

Once you've decided on a title, and you've watched it, so you're fully aware of its contents, you need to now buy it at its wholesale price. The best way to do this, while ensuring you're not buying something that has been pirated, is to buy it from a distributor. One reputable distributor that's been around for a long time is Video Products Distributors (VPD) at vpdinc.com There are very few requirements for opening an account with VPD, and their site lays it all out. For more sources, you can do an online search for "DVD distributors," being sure to scrutinize your findings carefully. Or, if you still have a Mom and Pop video store in your area, you can ask them who they would recommend.

Since there's such overlap, marketing DVDs will be discussed along with marketing books on the pages to follow.

STRATEGY NUMBER 2: Tie Into Books that Forward Your Mission

Amazon will come in handy again in your search for books. You can also go to Barnes and Noble, at barnesandnoble.com, abebooks.com, which is a repository for books sold around the world, or even visit an online book club like librarything.com or goodreads.com. Another good resource is the New York Times, at nytimes.com. There you'll find book reviews that date back to 1981. The site makes it easy to discover the books that have something to do with your cause, while also allowing you to see what the critics have to say about them.

Finding books is a simple enough process; in no time you should have a nice list. Naturally, you will want to read enough of them to make sure you feel comfortable offering them for sale, and so that you can offer an opinion of them.

The next step is to do some quick price comparisons. A site like bookfinder.com, that compares the prices of titles from multiple sites, makes this very easy to do. You then want to purchase copies of the book at a wholesale price. The easiest way to do that as a nonprofit organization is through Baker and Taylor (btol.com), one of the world's largest wholesalers. You will be buying books from the same wholesaler that's used by bookstores and libraries. To establish an account, call 800-775-1800, and press 6, or email them at btinfo@baker-taylor.com.

When you contact them let them know that you're a nonprofit, and they will set you up on the same type of account that they provide libraries, which means you can buy as many or as few books as you want—even one for that matter. After you set up an account with them they'll tell you your discount schedule, which should be 40 percent. They also carry DVD titles, giving you another reputable source for them.

Marketing Books and DVDs

The first step for marketing any product is to research prices so as to set a competitive price of your own. This is critical. You can't get away with the old nonprofit way of thinking on this, which is to sell items much higher than what they go for in the marketplace because it's tied to a cause. That's not going to work with this model. If Girl Scout cookies were $16 a box, it's doubtful that they would sell as well. So, make yourself competitive rather than pricing yourself out of the market.

The next step is to incorporate their sale into what you're currently doing. This will be repeated several times throughout this book, because it is the simplest most productive first step. Now, let's look at 10 additional marketing steps and techniques:

(1) Have your webmaster make a new page on your site for your books and DVDs, so you can start driving traffic to that page.

(2) If you currently give speeches, start getting permission from your host to offer your books and/or DVDs for sale at the back of the room following your presentation. A great way to showcase them is to hold a drawing, with the prize being the book or DVD you have to offer attendees. Midway through your speech ask, "How about I give something away?" Have attendees pull out their business cards to enter the drawing. In order to build your mailing list and to gain permission, say something like, "If you don't want to hear from us by email just write 'No Emails' on the back of your card and we'll honor that; otherwise, I'll subscribe you to our monthly e-letter."

Prior to pulling a name, take a few minutes to describe the item you're giving away. This is your chance to get people excited about buying a copy at the end of your talk, so do a good job of whetting their appetite.

By using a drawing, you showcase your items rather than sell them, and it feels better for everyone involved. During your talk, make a point of promising to email the audience a copy of something you've referenced, a resource of some kind. As soon as you get back to the office, enter the emails from the business cards you received into your database. Send out an email to attendees that serves the purpose of supplying them with the promised resource, and also to give them another chance to pick up a copy of the book or DVD. It's important that attendees receive this email the day after the presentation.

Tom Antion, a pioneer of this technique, consistently sells 20 percent of his audience a $5000 product by employing this technique. Imagine how successful you can be with a product that costs less than one percent of that price.

If you currently get booked for paid private speaking engagements you can include the books or DVDs in your quote. For example, if you have a book you sell for $20 you can provide 50 copies of it to attendees and increase your quote by $1000. One of three things will happen when you provide your quote: (1) you'll provide the quote and the person coordinating the event will be fine with it; (2) the coordinator will say the price is a bit out of their budget, at which time you say, "No problem, that price as you know includes 50 copies of the book *XYZ*, which I think is a must-read on the subject, but if it's not in your budget I'll remove the books and drop my price by $1000." Or, (3) the coordinator will say, "Well 50 copies is great but we're expecting 75 people, is it possible to buy an additional 25 more copies from you?" To which you say, "ABSOLUTELY!"

Apply the same strategy to your own events. Increase the price of fundraisers, conferences, or similar events by the retail price of your merchandise, and then advertise that the event includes a *Copy of XYZ.*

(3) If you have walk-in clients, display a copy of the book, or the DVD case with the DVD removed at the receptionist desk. Get a book easel for it, as shown below, and rotate out a new title on a regular basis to give your clients a chance to see your various titles.

Put a little tent card in front of it that lists its price. Also, put out a waiting room copy of the book. Attach a sticker on the front cover that says **Waiting Room Copy Do Not Remove.** Make sure you insert several order forms in the middle of the book. The receptionist's copy and the waiting room copy should be the same title, so that a person can make the connection that they can probably buy the book right on the spot.

If your clients pay a fee for service, teach your receptionist to casually ask the client when preparing the bill, "Would you like to include a copy of *XYZ* today for another $19.95?" Sure, the person sees the book there, sure, they see the price posted, and yes, they should be able to put together the fact that if they want the book they probably just need to ask, but there's something about actually being asked the question that makes the difference. So, help them by asking.

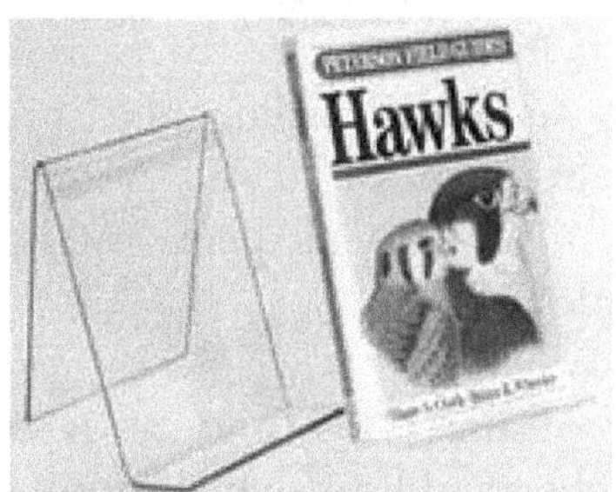

Book easel courtesy of displaystands4you.com

(4) If you currently staff a booth at street fairs, or the like, naturally you'll want to have your books and DVDs for sale there as well. If your booth is strictly a literature booth that restricts your ability to sell merchandise, bring a sample copy and take orders. Do something to incentivize ordering on the spot, bundling items for a discounted price, for example, and offering free shipping. Although you're collecting money, there's no

exchange of goods, so hopefully this will fall within the restrictions of a literature booth.

(5) If you currently have an e-letter, create a section that describes your latest acquisitions; you might name it something like the *Book Nook* or *The Reel Deal.* More important than its name is that the section provides a brief intriguing description of your titles. You should also make the last line somewhat of a cliff hanger:

> *From Prison to Paycheck: What No One Ever Tells You about Getting a Job* provides prisoners and formerly incarcerated individuals with the steps for navigating a job search with a criminal record. It explains how to discuss your conviction in an interview, and the importance of READ MORE.

The *Read More* link should be a direct link to the page that has the complete description and a link for buying the item. Don't send people to your homepage where they can get lost and distracted.

(6) If you currently send out mailings, be sure to enclose a one sheet describing your book or DVD. A one sheet is simply a marketing piece that supplies all pertinent information on one page. See the example below.

(7) Write a review of the book, and, as is customary, end the review with your website address, which should be a direct link to the book's page. Pay a high school student a nominal wage to post that review on the many sites that allow reviews. Here are 10 sites where you can post reviews, and there are certainly more out there: searchwarp.com, viewpoints.com, articlecube.com, lunch.com, ezinearticles.com, goodreads.com, bookwormr.com, librarything.com, articledashboard.com, and books.vjad.net. By posting reviews, you're meeting people where they are and you're helping them find you. They click over to your site and they find your information, and they also see that you sell the book at a competitive price.

Overcoming Angst and Alienation: Arthur's Story

Growing up is no easy task... but try doing it after a near-death experience ***and*** the death of your father.

Arthur Newman, the new kid at Skyview High, battles hormones, bullies, alienation, depression, and personal life issues - all while trying to discover the "real" Arthur.

In Adam Dustus' new release, ***High School Asylum***, readers experience the ups and downs of puberty and high school life, while watching Arthur develop into an unlikely hero.

High School Asylum is about more than just growing pains - it addresses the psychological impact of a teenager's struggles. Arthur finds an outlet for his angst and personal loss, while shattering expectations.

ISBN 0-7414-5151-4
Infinity Publishing May 4, 2009
374 Pages
$18.95
Coming soon to Barnesandnoble.com and Walmart.com

Author and poet, Adam Dustus, brings a fresh new voice to the world of literature. His debut novel ***High School Asylum***, and his poetic publication ***In & Out of Line***, were published May 2009. Dustus' writing career began at The University of Tennessee, the liberal arts program proudly acknowledged by its notable literary alumnus Cormac McCarthy. His second novel, ***Sounds From A House*** will be released summer 2009.

For additional information or to arrange an interview, contact:
Patricia F. Klier, Public Relations Manager
Prguide@prpr.net, 800-786-1764

Sample of a one sheet

This marketing technique can help you serve people who you might not otherwise reach. Imagine a young woman researching breast cancer treatments. She wants to see what's being said about the drug Tamoxifin. She goes to Google and searches on Tamoxifin, and a review for Susan Love's book *Breast Cancer Survival* comes up. She reads the review and clicks on the accompanying link, which takes her to the website for an organization called *A Place for Women*. There she finds a few books for sale on the topic of breast cancer, including Susan Love's book. Even though this young lady has no need for the organization's services at this time, she has a need for their books. And, that is the beauty of meeting people where they are.

(8) Once you have several items for sale you can create a simple catalog. You might want to offset the cost of printing and postage by selling ad space in the catalog. Make it a requirement that ads are submitted to you in camera ready form, so that they don't require any work on your part. If you offer exclusivity, i.e., only one professional to a field, this has more value to an advertiser, and your rates should reflect that. In lieu of ads, or in addition to them, you can sell advertorial space.

An advertorial is an advertisement written in the form of an objective article. They read like instructive pieces, which is why it's customary to note at the top of them that it's advertising, as shown below. Businesses like advertorials because they tend to pull better than ads. Again, the business provides the advertorial in camera ready form.

Be sure not to downplay the value of the space for sale in your catalog. Catalogs offer advantages over other forms of advertising. First of all, catalogs get passed around, which means that they have both a primary audience, the person you intended the catalog to go to, as well as a pass-along audience, all of the unintended viewers of the ad, like other members of the household or co-workers. This increases the ad's potential for impressions, i.e., people exposed to the ad. Let's say you do a mailing to 500 of your stakeholders. With the pass along audience the number of

HYDROXATONE®
HEALTHNEWS

ADVERTISEMENT

Erase Wrinkles Without Botox®*!

*Breakthrough anti-aging cream combines three scientifically advanced wrinkle-reducing ingredients to rival the results of Botox®**.

In recent years Botox®* has been promoted as the leader of anti-wrinkle treatments. Although it can be successful, it is very expensive, painful, must be administered by a physician, and, in many cases, two to three treatments are needed for the desired corrections. After years of research and testing, a new safe, more affordable product offering comparable results is now available.

What Our Customers Have To Say About Hydroxatone®...

"Within two weeks of using Hydroxatone®, I was getting compliments on my skin from friends and co-workers. My skin not only feels great, but it looks great too! You've made me a Hydroxatone® believer!"

— Robin B., Los Angeles

Why Choose Hydroxatone®			
PRODUCT	Hydroxatone®	Olay® Regenerist	StriVectin SD®
Argireline®	YES	NO	NO
Matrixyl™ 3000®	YES	NO	NO
Hyaluronic Acid	YES	NO	NO

Most Advanced Anti-Aging Product Available

Hydroxatone® is a true, clinically proven Botox®* alternative. It is a superior facial cream that can reduce deep wrinkles, and it's completely non-toxic, safe and has no side effects. How can it rival Botox®*? Hydroxatone® contains three of the most effective substances known that are needed for real results. Most products use one or two of these important ingredients, but the makers of Hydroxatone® are the first to combine all three, resulting in the most advanced skin care and wrinkle reducer on the market.

Three Proven Wrinkle-Reducing Ingredients

Hydroxatone® is unlike any other skin cream you've ever tried because it relies on THREE proven ingredients for REAL results. Matrixyl™ 3000® is clinically proven to promote collagen production in the skin. Collagen is the most powerful substance known to help keep skin stay young, soft and vibrant. Argireline®* is a combination of amino acids formulated to relax facial wrinkles, reduce the degree of existing wrinkles and stop their future development. And Hyaluronic Acid is virtually unmatched in hydrating the skin, resulting in increased smoothness, softening, elasticity and decreased facial wrinkles. But Hydroxatone® doesn't stop there! It also includes other natural antioxidants, botanicals, vitamins, and peptides and a gentle but powerful exfoliant...all to nourish your skin while fading wrinkles.

Up To 68% Reduction Of Deep Wrinkles

Unless you've actually tried Hydroxatone®, it's hard to imagine it can work the miracles users claim it does. But women and men of all ages are using Hydroxatone® and seeing real and noticeable results every day. The cumulative results that are seen within two weeks will continue with daily use. Over six months this will increase to as much as a 68% reduction in deep wrinkles.

There Is No Comparison

Forget Botox®* or any other radical treatments. Throw out other creams that simply don't work. Hydroxatone® is a proven anti-wrinkle cream that is completely safe and clinically proven. Within two weeks Hydroxatone® users will start to see results. With continued use, their skin will become softer, smoother, more radiant, and younger-looking...and that's GUARANTEED.

HOW Hydroxatone® WORKS

MATRIXYL™ 3000® + ARGIRELINE® + HYALURONIC ACID

- 68% reduction of deep wrinkles in just six months
- Diminished age spots & increased suppleness
- Enhanced production of healthy, radiant new skin
- Tightened and toned skin

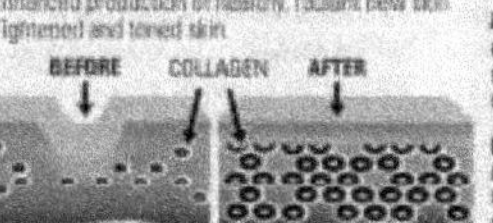

Matrixyl™ 3000® – is clinically proven to promote collagen production in the skin.

Argireline® – is a combination of amino acids formulated to relax facial wrinkles, reduce the degree of existing wrinkles and stop their future development.

Hyaluronic Acid – is virtually unmatched in hydrating the skin, resulting in increased smoothness, softening, elasticity and decreased facial wrinkles.

Having A Hard Time Finding Hydroxatone®?

For years consumers have only had expensive and ineffective alternatives to achieve younger looking skin. You may have seen other inferior anti-wrinkle products costing hundreds of dollars at some high priced salons. Unlike those pricey and unproven alternatives, the manufacturer of Hydroxatone® is so confident in their anti-aging technology that they are offering a 30-day risk free trial offer... because seeing is believing!

To get your supply of Hydroxatone® risk free, for just a small S&H fee call 888-409-2409. Our operators are available to let you try one of the greatest breakthroughs in wrinkle fighting technology without spending hundreds of dollars.

Call 888-409-2409 to get your Hydroxatone® 30-Day Risk Free Trial Offer Today! Mention Promotion Code 2HLH11C for a Free Upgrade!

www.hydroxatonedirect.com

Sample Advertorial

impressions could be 1000 or even 1,500 people, and this is the number your ad rep should quote. Also, people tend to hold onto catalogs for a while, which in advertising means that they have a high shelf life, higher than a newspapers, for example. And lastly, you would be mailing these catalogs to people who already know, like, and trust you, i.e., a warm list. This is also appealing to an advertiser, because the response rate to warm lists is typically better than cold mailings.

Give some thought to these advertising factors as you set a price for advertising in your catalog. Once you come up with a price, double it, and use that number as your starting price from which advertisers can haggle. Being a small catalog you won't want to overdo the ads. An experienced salesperson should be able to sell all of your spaces in two or three days.

9) Make them an offer they can't refuse. What if I said, "When you order your copy of *Beautiful Boy: A Father's Journey through his Sons Addiction* for $15 you will also get a free copy of the booklet *What the Government Doesn't Want You to Know about Meth*, a one gigabyte memory stick, and a pocket day planner." Wouldn't you say, "Well gee, the book sells for $15 at Amazon, but it's not like I'm going to get this other stuff if I buy it from them, what the heck?" Sure you would.

Now, to make this work you need to get gift items that don't cost you anything. Finding companies willing to give you free promotional items is a simple task. If you've ever gone to a tradeshow, you've seen how common it is for companies to give away all sorts of personalized items to attendees who spend a minute at their booth. If so, then you know that this request is a no-brainer. After all, you're doing them a favor by getting their personalized merchandise into the hands of people they want to reach. Staying with the example of the book about addiction, you could just do an online search on the term "drug treatment centers."

You would then need to call a few of the centers and tell them what your organization does, and say something to the effect of:

> The reason I'm calling is because we're resellers of books about addiction, and I was wondering if you might have any booklets about addiction, or any merchandise that's personalized with your center's name on it, that you'd like to have distributed to buyers of our books?

And then wait a second as the person recovers from their shock at how great an offer you just made them. When you agree on an item and are asked how many you need, don't be shy:

You: Well, I want to make it as easy on you as possible, how many come in a box?

Company Rep: I think 100.

You: Well then, why don't you just send me a box.

One company may give you enough variety to be set, if not, call another until you have at least two or three freebies. Maintain the relationship so that you can return as needed. If you build a handful of these kinds of relationships, you'll never be at a loss for gifts you can use to encourage people to buy from you, whether at a street fair or through your website.

And remember, people like the *idea* of free stuff as much as the stuff itself, so don't worry if your freebies aren't magic beans. Just write it up well. For example, notice above, it wasn't just a memory stick, it was a one gigabyte memory stick. Were it the type of memory stick that was on a keychain you should say as much, "a one gigabyte keychain memory stick." You get the idea.

(10) When you fill orders, enclose two things with the shipment, both of which are designed to help you build upon your budding relationship: (1) enclose a one sheet, or a sales sheet, or a catalog

to display the other books and/or DVDs you have, and (2) enclose a special thank you letter.

If we stay with the organization that addresses drug abuse as an example, their thank you letter might say something like this:

> The XYZ organization is committed to bringing awareness to the prevalence of meth addiction, and we believe this book does an excellent job of portraying the damaging effects of meth on users and family members alike.
>
> By purchasing this book through our organization you have supported our efforts, and for that we would like to thank you with a **SPECIAL GIFT**.
>
> Please visit our website at addictionrealities.org/report for a free copy of the Special Report *10 Steps for Identifying Addictive Personalities.*
>
> Again, thank you for your support.

Have your webmaster set up an opt-in box on that page that requires visitors provide their email address to receive the report. You have no doubt seen such boxes enough times to correctly conclude that they are a very effective way to build an email list.

By using opt-in boxes, you will develop a list of people who have demonstrated an interest in the topic covered by your books and other media. With a list like this, you will be able to generate sales with one email blast. We will refer back to this list-building technique several times throughout the book.

TIM PAULSON
CHANGES LIVES !

For a FREE "Business Success Secrets" Confidential Report From Tim Paulson, simply fill in the form below...

* Name:

* Email:

submit

timpaulson.com

joepolish.com

Claim Your FREE Special Report Right Now!

Fill out the form below and you'll immediately receive a "Boost Your Metabolism" and learn first hand how **easy it is to BURN THE FAT** and start having the body you want right now!

Enter Your First Name:

Type In Your Email Address:

boostyourmetabolism.com

Download our
FREE AUDIO-WEB E-BOOK **"THE BOOK ON INTERNET AUDIO"** &
FREE PRODUCTION MUSIC!
by joining our opt-in email list!

Name

Email

Claim Your Ebook & FREE Music

internetaudioguy.com

Examples of opt-in boxes from various websites

STRATEGY NUMBER 3: Personalize Merchandise with Messages Aligned with Your Cause

In this Internet era, nothing could be easier than creating and generating income from marketing personalized merchandise. There are sites online that exist for the sole purpose of helping you design, display, and ultimately sell your merchandise. One such place is cafepress.com. They allow printing on a wide variety of items, from clothing to mouse pads, buttons and magnets, to aprons, clocks, calendars, journals, baby bibs, and pet bowls. You can purchase the items in bulk with as few as six, and as your numbers increase, so does your bulk discount, topping out at 45 percent. You can also sell your items through their marketplace, which means you design your product, it gets listed on their site, and when people browse their site and buy your stuff, CafePress ships it out and sends you a commission check.

Two other sites that do the same thing are customink.com and zazzle.com. You can actually print an image on a real U.S. postage stamp at Zazzle. Now, how's that for getting creative? People have to buy stamps anyway, why not a stamp with your organization's logo or message on it? There is also districtlines.com and spreadshirt.com where they only sell clothes.

Online establishments like these allow you to print one item at a time, which is nice for testing the waters. But, once you start getting positive feedback from an item, you should compare prices with more traditional operations to make sure you're getting the best price. For example, take a look at B&F Systems at bnfusa.com and stamonline.com. They have a ton of merchandise to choose from at very good prices.

Marketing and Selling your Merchandise

It's nice to be able to take advantage of the traffic places like

CafePress have, but you should definitely have your webmaster create a page on your site dedicated to your merchandise as well.

Utilize offline marketing also. Whenever you send out a mailing, enclose an insert that serves as both an advertisement and an order form. You might also have some bookmarks printed that advertise your items. Bookmarks are functional which gives people a reason to hold on to them, and you can print 1000 of them for under $30. But the beauty of bookmarks is that you can get a volunteer to drop off a stack at bookstores or libraries to provide them to patrons, free for the taking. GotPrint.com is a great resource for high quality printing of this kind at very affordable prices.

You don't want to spend your time selling merchandise; instead, spend some time brainstorming on ways that other people can move merchandise for you. To follow are a few ways to accomplish that.

Depending on the merchandise and what you have printed on it, you can consider selling it through local merchants that sell complementary products. The beauty of what you're doing is that you are monetizing your mission, which means the message and the income stream are more important than the merchandise. So, come up with the message first and then think strategically about the merchandise to print it on. For example, let's say you have an eco-friendly message, if you print that message on a bicycle water bottle, a bicycle shop might be willing to sell your item, at least on a consignment basis.

To sell to retailers, of course, requires that you buy the item at a price that allows you to make a profit after selling it to a merchant at a price that allows them to also make a profit. If a retailer's sales take off you will be able to buy in larger quantities, which should mean getting the merchandise at a better price.

You can also create a business opportunity that involves selling your items. Individuals would put down a deposit on your merchandise and go into the neighborhood to sell it. They might set up a table in a busy area, or go door-to-door to homes or retail establishments.

If you have multiple items, they can put the merchandise in a nice simple box and go into places like beauty salons, car washes, and nail salons, places where people are sitting around with time on their hands, and present the items they have for sale. Items priced in the $25 range and below are easy to sell in this way. This direct sales technique has been used by companies for decades.

To assess the income potential, we'll use an item that retails for $25 that cost you $8 to buy wholesale. If you pay your reps $10 a sale you net $7. With just 10 reps selling 30 items a week each, which is typical for this kind of work, for a total of 300 sales per week, you would net $2,100 a week, or over $100,000 a year. Clearly, 10 reps are just the tip of the iceberg. By setting the deposit at, or slightly above, your wholesale cost you incur no loss if the rep skips out on you with the merchandise.

Another sales method is reminiscent of the Avon book or the 5k sponsor sheet that gets circulated in an office. A salesperson walks into an office and asks the receptionist if it's okay to leave behind a sample of an item and an order form and to allow it to circulate for a day, promising to retrieve both the following day. It's best to leave a sample of the item, but if it's too large for that to be feasible, then a picture and description will do.

The order form, which you can see an example of below, simply needs to accommodate a buyer's name, the quantity ordered, and their method of payment. The form is stapled to the front of a manila envelope.

$20 OR 2 for $35 Make checks payable to: Save the Whales or Enclose Cash			
Name	Check #	Amount of Cash Enclosed	Quantity Ordered

For Future Orders Call: 987-654-3210

As the sample and form circulate, buyers put a check or cash inside the envelope and fill out the form. The sales rep returns the following day, retrieves the sample and payment, leaves the quantity of items indicated on the order sheet, and returns the order sheet to the receptionist so she knows who ordered what. In a matter of minutes, the rep is off to the next office in the building. This approach is so easy that even people who really aren't salespeople can be successful at it.

For more marketing strategies, revisit those discussed for marketing books and DVDs.

STRATEGY NUMBER 4: Compile a CD or DVD of Compelling Stories

There are a few moving parts involved in producing and marketing a CD of compelling stories, so we'll take it one step at a time. An audio CD holds 80 minutes, although experts recommend keeping your recording closer to 72. So, unless you want to do a multiple CD program, keep this in mind when choosing the number of stories you want to capture. Let's dive into this strategy.

Storytellers and Interviews

Put out a call for storytellers through an email blast to your stakeholders that explains the project. Having interested parties contact you by phone will allow you to screen people who you believe will best serve the project in a way that email responses can't do. After you find your storytellers, you'll need to start preparing for the interview. You should have your questions written out so that you will be sure to ask the same questions of everyone you interview. This will make it easy to identify the common themes the stories share, which could provide some interesting motifs for the piece. Although you want to find people who can tell their story fluidly, you also should be prepared to ask probing questions that will tease the story out further and which will get your storytellers to go deeper than they might otherwise go.

You want to interview with a mind towards getting the finished product you desire, and with editing in mind. Good stories have as much to do with good editing as they do with the storyteller and the story itself. You can't expect that someone is going to come in and tell a story in a way that hits all the marks. If you find yourself confused or not following the story very well, you need to jump in there and ask a clarifying question, or get the person to back up a bit and start again.

Here are two interviewing tips. First, remember that people tend to answer questions without repeating aloud the question. For example, if you ask, "Mike, what was the hardest part about making it on your own after aging out of foster care?" He's likely to say something like, "Getting a job." Now, if Mike answers all of your questions like this, it forces you to include the interviewer's voice in the piece. And, that's not necessarily a bad thing, but with answers like that you won't have any other choice but to do so. So, before you start the interview you want to instruct Mike to include your question in his answers, so that instead of answering, "getting a job" he answers, "the hardest part about aging out of foster care was getting a job."

This second tip will make editing easier. Give your storytellers a place to reenter the story when they go off track. If a person is rambling down a road and you're saying to yourself, "Man, I'm going to have to cut out all of this," make it easy on yourself by not only redirecting the person, but by giving them a jumping off point that you can use during editing. So, here's rambling Mike: "Getting a job was tough because I didn't know what went into a resume or what a cover letter was, or how to make one. I guess I could have asked for help, but as my friends always tell me, I'm stubborn. I guess I get that from my father, I mean I didn't know him very well, I mean I really didn't know him at all. But before my mother got sick she used to tell me that I was like him, that is before. . . ."

Okay, clearly we need to bring Mike back to the question. Now, if you just say, "Hey Mike, snap out of it!" he may not start back at the beginning of his point. So direct him back with, "So, you were saying you could have asked for help, how's that?" When he answers, "I could have asked a career advisor at school for help," you've given yourself a spot that will work well for editing. You'll be able to delete the ramblings and use this response as a lead-in back to the story.

Recording a CD

These days the equipment exists for you to create your own private recording studio in your office. And, right now I'm going to walk you through some tips for doing that, and you can then bring in someone knowledgeable who can act as your engineer. On the other hand, you can go into a studio and record there. Studio rates range from $60 to $120 an hour. The rate has a lot to do with whether you're talking about a spare room in someone's house with egg cartons for soundproofing, or a professional outfit with a highly experienced engineer at the ready.

To make a good recording you absolutely must use a studio quality microphone. A microphone that is also a USB mic, meaning it plugs directly into a USB port in your computer, is ideal. The Audio-Technica AT2020 USB Condenser Microphone fits the bill. It has a large diaphragm condenser that gives it studio quality, and it plugs directly into your computer. It's a $250 microphone that now sells for under $100 at places like Amazon and musiciansfriend.com. You should also buy a pop filter. This is a screen that goes in front of the microphone to prevent the popping sound that occurs when words that carry a lot of air are spoken into it. Pop filters start at $14.

Lastly, you will need software that will allow you to record and edit your audio on your computer. Sony Sound Forge is a popular easy to use recording and editing software program made for the PC. The one you want is in the $50 range, not the more expensive one for musicians. If you use a Mac, you no doubt have the latest recording application already installed on your computer, which should suffice. There is also a free open source software program for recording and editing called Audacity, which is available at audacity.sourceforge.net

Equipped with a good microphone, a pop filter, and software you need a quiet place for recording. Take a minute to listen to the sounds of any room you're considering using before you deem it suitable for recording in. Plug in your mic before launching your software, you can then go into the software program and select your microphone as your audio device preference. You should then go into your computer's control panel to adjust your microphone's volume. Do a test run of your sound, using the software's channel meters to monitor your sound levels. You want to stay between -12dB and -6dB when recording.

Saving Recordings

It's important to make a point of keeping your original version in its raw unedited state, just in case you rethink your edits or want to take the project in a different direction. You may even want to use the material for something else down the road. If you keep your original recording intact you will have these options available to you.

Editing

Editing audio is very similar to editing words in a word processing program like Microsoft Word, you simply highlight your audio, much as you would in Word, and hit delete. Likewise, you can cut and paste audio just as you would text.

If you take some time to familiarize yourself with the tutorials that accompany your recording and editing software you will quickly see how easy it is to edit your recordings. If this isn't for you, you should have no trouble finding someone to do this for you by simply looking on craigslist (craigslist.com), if it serves your area. Make it easy on the editor, whether that ends up being you or someone else, by making a distinct loud noise, like a clap, into the microphone whenever a mistake occurs and it's followed by a second take. The sound will show up as a big spike in the line of audio and will alert the editor that a cut is needed in that area.

By inserting markers you can put tracks on your CD. Tracks allow your listeners to jump from story to story, but more importantly it prevents them from having to start at the beginning of the CD every time they stop the recording, or if their hand slips while rewinding. After editing is complete, you're ready to burn a master which you will use for duplication.

Duplication - Yourself

You can duplicate CDs yourself, using your computer's CD burner, or an external one that plugs into it. You'll need to buy blank CD-Rs. A CD-R is not rewriteable, you get one use out of them, whereas CD-RWs are reusable, which makes them inappropriate for your project. You will be putting labels on your CDs so be sure to buy CDs that don't have printing on their face; otherwise, it will show through the label. One resource for buying discs is polylinecorp.com There are differences among manufacturers, so going with a name brand is better than going with the cheapest option.

To label your CDs, you will need a labeler like *Sure Thing CD Labeler* found at surething.com. This is a tried and tested program that continues to surpass the competition. Also, their labels are about half the price of the major competition, and they have a slew of label backgrounds to choose from.

Duplication - Outsourced

You can also choose to send your program out for duplication. The quality of CD duplication has become pretty standard over the years, which means you should be able to find someone local and save on shipping. You may also use on demand duplication at a place like Kunaki, at kunaki.com. Although their prices are competitive, you should compare them with a local brick and mortar establishment, especially after you start duplicating large quantities.

You can also choose to have Kunaki fulfill your orders. You can either take orders on your site and provide Kunaki with the purchaser's address, and they'll drop ship the product for you, or you can set it up so that orders go straight to them for fulfillment, and they will send you a check at the end of the month.

As promised, there are a few moving parts to creating a CD of stories, but also as discussed there are many options. You can do it all yourself, do none of it yourself, or something in between. There are a few options for duplication as well. However you choose to go about the production of your CD, the most important thing is that in the end you're going to have a great product that will generate income for years to come.

Recording a DVD

When it comes to creating a high quality DVD of compelling stories, the simplest approach that promises the best results worthy of a commercial price is to hire a videographer and editor. Using professionals, however, doesn't have to break the bank, and we'll discuss costs shortly.

Again, if craigslist serves your area, you should be able to do a search for *videographer* in the Small Biz Ads section and get a nice list to choose from. Expand your search outside of your city if you need a bigger selection, since videographers are used to traveling to get to their gigs.

Check out each videographer's work, not only for quality, but to make sure that their experience matches your project. Don't use a guy whose experience is in shooting wildlife, or who touts outdoor experience if your project involves an inside shoot. Why? Because you need someone experienced lighting subjects, and someone who primarily shoots outdoors isn't that guy. Lighting is one of the most critical elements for obtaining a professionally produced look. Even a wedding videographer isn't necessarily experienced at lighting subjects, since he's used to making do with the surroundings he's presented with. But, you can be sure that most videographers will promise that they can achieve the results you're after. Don't buy it. Keep looking. By scrutinizing their ad, viewing the clips they provide on their website, and having a phone conversation with them that entails determining where their experience lies, it shouldn't be hard to find a videographer who's a good match for your project.

The rate for hiring a videographer should be somewhere between $500-$900 for an eight-hour day. Your videographer is going to make this project pretty simple for you. You'll just need to focus on what it is you want to capture for your piece. That's your job. If you're 100 percent clear about what you want to achieve you'll get it. When you're paying someone to run a camera you don't want to be figuring this out on the fly. You'll save time and money if you use one location. So, it makes sense to have your subjects come to your office, unless their environments have as much to do with the story as the story itself. Don't worry if your office is small, a good camera person can work magic with limited space, especially for interviews, because the shots are in so tight on the subject.

Compensation

When it comes to choosing storytellers, again, make sure the initial phone screening convinces you that they are the right people for the project. If it feels otherwise you should trust that feeling. You need to decide if you're going to pay your storytellers or make receiving a copy of the finished product the entire compensation. If you pay your storytellers, make it a nominal fee and don't list it in any ads or mention it early in the phone screening. You want people motivated by the project not by the money, because these are the people who will work the hardest to make sure the project is a success. Therefore, let it be a red flag if one of the first questions asked by someone is how much they're going to be paid. If you do pay your storytellers, be sure to make it a flat rate, you want them incentivized to do a good job as quickly as possible.

You should have your subjects sign a Name and Likeness Release statement before the camera starts rolling. Your legal person can draft something for you, but it's basically a simple one page document that gives you consent to record, use and reuse the person's voice, actions, likeness, name, appearance and biographical materials in any and all media now known or hereafter devised, throughout the universe, in perpetuity, in or in connection with your program. It gives you permission to use all or any part of the person's likeness and to alter or modify it. It also should state that you own all the rights, title, and interest to the material. A release also allows you to use the likeness for promotion, publicity, marketing or advertisement for the Program or for any other purpose and manner whatsoever.

Editing

You will also need an editor. Some videographers edit their own work. The busy ones don't have time to do their own editing, but they tend to work in tandem with an editor, or they should be able to recommend one. A good editor can charge $150 an hour. It may come as a surprise, but you will no doubt end up paying your editor more money than your videographer because editing is very time consuming. You won't have any way of knowing exactly how much time it will take until you finish shooting, because editing involves removing mistakes and connecting the adjoining pieces with smooth transitions.

You can save a great deal of money by getting involved in the editing process. If you take the time to review the raw footage and provide the editor with notes, you can save your editor a significant amount of time. And, it's very easy to do this.

First, have your videographer tell you where to go to have window dubs made. This is a process that overlays time codes onto a copy of the footage. The cost for this is about $20-$40 per video. With time codes displayed at the bottom of the video, you will simply need to watch the footage and make a note of the time code displayed where you find a mistake. You should create a page like the one below to make things simple. When you come across a mistake, you note on the sheet the time code and the words spoken or picture displayed at that time. In the example below, an editor can see that you want to delete footage that falls after 02:05:27, and that you want to come back in at 02:05:49, and let it run until 02:06:03. With your edits outlined in this way, an editor would simply need to find the footage indicated by the time code you provided, confirm that your description matches what's on the screen, and make the cut.

Description	Time Code In	Time Code Out
Let's talk about what it takes to get a job with a record . . .	02:04:54	
. . . . and that is the last thing you should do.		02:05:27
Are you prepared to answer questions about gaps . . .	02:05:49	
. . . . you give the interviewer all the power.		02:06:03

Sample Editing Sheet

As stated earlier, handling a lot of footage is time consuming, so even if you provide your editor with this kind of direction, each hour of the final product can require five times that for editing. So, for example, if your final product is a two hour DVD, you could easily have 10 hours of editing on your hands, even with you providing an editing sheet. But, 10 hours is clearly better than 30.

Duplication

When it comes to duplicating your DVDs there are a lot of variables, so you want to get someone who knows what they're doing. When you get your copies, you want to test them on various machines to make sure they play correctly.

For duplication on the large scale, there's Discmakers, at discmakers.com. On the smaller Mom and Pop scale, there's Command Productions (commandproductions.com) at 415-332-3161. They may be small, but they work with some big names and they do good work. They're also very accessible, and they don't have a minimum order requirement, as many of the larger places do, so they're a good place to launch this strategy. Their website doesn't do a good job of representing their quality of work or reputation. It's probably best to just pick up the phone and give them a call. Your videographer may also have some local suggestions as well.

Marketing CDs and DVDs of Compelling Stories

Okay, so now you have this CD or DVD of amazing stories that you want to get out to the public and start generating revenue with. You may already have a ton of ideas on how to market it. Some marketing suggestions discussed for other items you'll want to incorporate for media as well, such as:

- Display its empty case at the receptionist counter.
- Have it for sale at the back of the room of your speaking engagements.
- Include its retail price in your quote for private speaking engagements.
- Sell it at street fairs.
- Include it in the price of your fundraiser tickets.

But, now that we're talking about a product that you own the rights to you're also able to do things you wouldn't be able to do for a book or DVD you didn't create. You can't exactly go on radio shows to promote someone else's product. But, now that you have your own product you can do exactly that. If you've ever been a guest on a radio show you already know how easy it is, and that they're primarily done by telephone these days. You may or may not know, however, how important guests are to radio shows. They couldn't do what they do without you. In fact, radio stations need 10,000 guests per day! So, although it's easy to feel like you need *them*; in fact, the feeling is mutual. And, radio is the perfect outlet to promote your CDs and DVDs of compelling stories, as proven by Jack Canfield and Mark Victor Hansen, creators of the *Chicken Soup for the Soul* series. They attribute their ability to sell 80 million copies of the series to being a guest on radio shows across the country. Now, what is the *Chicken Soup for the Soul* series? A compilation of compelling stories. What is your CD or DVD? A compilation of compelling stories, which is why being a guest on radio shows is something you should consider seriously. A radio show allows you to share your message. You talk about the problem your organization works to combat or solve, and you share a story or two that they can hear more of by buying a copy of your program.

You want an easy site name to say on the radio, which means you don't want to get into forward slashes. And remember, there's no longer any need to lumber through the *www* when referencing a site. An easy way to get your listeners to the page you want while still having a simple website name is to buy a memorable domain name, and to have your webmaster redirect that name so that it goes to the desired page. The redirection is instantaneous and virtually imperceptible. This allows you to say on the radio, "listeners can hear a sample of the program by going to fosterstories.com," when in fact you're actually sending them to helpingourfosteryouth.com/theirstories.

A great resource for learning how to get booked on radio shows, and for a list of the largest radio stations in the country is Alex Carroll. He has sold over a million and a half dollars worth of books as a result of being a guest on over 1,000 radio shows. He admits to doing some of his early morning interviews while still lying in bed. If you visit his site, radiopublicity.com, you can get a free copy of the contact information for the top 20 nationally syndicated radio talk shows. Or, you can invest in his program and get a complete directory as well as step-by-step instructions for getting booked.

STRATEGY NUMBER 5: Offer Support Products That Serve the Needs of Your Stakeholders

The support products you choose to sell will be those you determine your stakeholders need. Whatever those items turn out to be, you will want to buy them, not at a bulk discount, but at a wholesale price. To find anything at a wholesale price online, you just type into a search engine the word *wholesale* and the item you're trying to find, for example, *wholesale blood pressure monitors.*

If Google gives you more discount retailers than actual wholesalers, use Alta Vista at altavista.com, (yes, Alta Vista still exists) or Ask.com. If you know the name of the company or product just go to Alta Vista and do a general search. In addition, here are three wholesale sources that may prove useful: Thomasnet.com, wholesalecentral.com, and closeoutcentral.com. Between doing general searches and utilizing these resources you should have no trouble whatsoever finding and obtaining items at a wholesale price.

Marketing Your Support Products

Don't just quietly start selling support products. Spread the word. If you have walk-in clients, get a banner made up from a Kinkos or somewhere that says:

Or, if feasible, state the product. Put this banner up in a prominent place somewhere in your office. Take it to street fairs.

Have flyers or sales bulletins printed that display the products and their prices, and put these at the front desk for your walk-in visitors. If there's room at the receptionist counter, or somewhere else that gets client traffic, make a product display. Take the empty product boxes and make a small pyramid out of them. Tape all of the boxes together, taping the bottom box to the desk so that they're all secure and can't be toppled. Do whatever it takes to reach your walk-in clients.

Online Marketing

Send out an email blast to spread the word, something along the lines of:

> In an effort to better serve your needs, the XYZ Center is proud to announce that effective (use yesterday's date) we will begin selling support products.
>
> You will now be able to purchase your A and B and C from the Center you have come to know and trust over the years. We will always offer you the most competitive price available.
>
> For your convenience, you can obtain your items when visiting the office, or you can order them over the phone, or online.
>
> We are also very interested in hearing your ideas about other products we can assist you with. Why not take a moment right now to see if there's anything we've forgotten LINK.

It's always a good idea to give folks a reason to visit your site other than the obvious reason, which is to buy your products. By asking readers to see if there's anything you've forgotten, in a sense you're saying, "go over to our site and see if you can spot our mistakes." It's compelling.

Additional Marketing Techniques

In addition to the email blast, you should also call your stakeholders. If you're already set up with a phone bank of some kind that volunteers help with, fantastic. If not, you can put out a call for volunteers to help out, whether from home with local numbers or from the office, if you can accommodate them. Provide them all with a script and a deadline for completing the calls, so that everyone is notified within the same window of time.

It's best to make calls in addition to sending emails, because email will reach some and not others. We also know that receiving emails is one thing, while opening and reading emails is another. A call helps to ensure that you really have gotten the word out; it's fine if this means some people will hear about it twice.

The purpose of the phone call should not just be to make sure the caller has heard the news about what you are now offering, but to get the caller involved by asking if there's any other items they would like to see added to the list, and finally, to ask if there's anything the caller is currently in need of. Be sure to teach your volunteers how to take orders.

Once again, you want to get the word out using all of your typical outlets as well. So, whatever mailings you tend to do you will want to be sure to enclose a sales bulletin. If you do street fairs, sell your products there if allowed. Lastly, if you send out an end of year letter, be sure to mention how this year marked the launch of your product offerings.

An even better way to utilize your end of year letter is to take a page out of the book of public broadcasting's pledge drives and incentivize donations with a thank you gift. Let's say your end of year letters typically result in people giving between $25 and $50. Incentivize making a $75 donation by offering one of your lower priced support items as a thank you gift. And, give donors of $125 a choice between gift A or gift B. A $200 donation might include both gift A and B, or just one much nicer item. Do the math on this to be sure to find the right donation levels and products to offer, but you get the idea.

Even if very few readers donate enough to receive a thank you gift, you have found another way to graciously showcase your products. You can also use your books, CDs, DVDs, and personalized merchandise in this way as well.

STRATEGY NUMBER 6: Produce Special Reports

Producing special reports is as simple as writing a few pages of quality content on a subject your stakeholders have demonstrated an interest in learning more about, and putting the document in the marketplace. Dan Poynter, Joan Stewart, and Marketing Sherpa demonstrate how people are using special reports on various topics to generate income.

Locating the Right Distributor describes how the book industry works. Then it describes more than 80 book trade distributors and lists the types of books each specializes in. This Instant Report will help you locate the right distributor for your book or line of books. Resources with addresses, telephone numbers and fax numbers. 11 pages.
ISBN: Document 605
Cover Price: $13.95
Self-Service Electronic Price: $9.95

Download Now! Order Now!

Selling Books through the Gift Trade. Lists the resources you need to reach gift shows, magazines, mailing lists, reports and consultants. 5 pages
ISBN: Document 614
Cover Price: $10.95
Self-Service Electronic Price: $6.95

Download Now! Order Now!

Selling Books to Catalogs. Catalogs buy books in large quantities and they are committed to you for the life of the catalog, often more than a year. This report shows you how to find the right catalogs out of more than 7,000, how to submit to them and how to deal with them. Be prepared to order another print run. 5 pages.
ISBN: Document 625
Cover Price: $12.95
Self-Service Electronic Price: $8.95

Special reports for sale at parapublishing.com

Dan Poynter (parapublishing.com) sells reports on self-publishing. Notice above that the digital version of some of his five-page reports sell for $6.95 and $8.95, while the print version sells for $10.95 and $12.95 respectively.

All of Joan Stewart's (publicityhound.com) reports on publicity sell for $15, some of which are five pages long.

Special Report #1: Damage Control: How to Keep the Media from Making a Mess of Your Story

Special Report #2: Questions You Can Expect Reporters to Ask During an Interview

Special Report #3: How to Use Free Publicity to Attract and Keep Qualified Employees

Special reports sold at publicityhound.com

Order Here Risk-Free

Social Media Benchmark Report
PDF + Print

Price: $447

Add to Cart

or

Social Media Benchmark Report
PDF ONLY

Price: $397

Add to Cart

The 2010 Social Media Marketing Benchmark Report includes:

- 197 charts and tables
- 14 chapters and 255 pages
- Research from 2,317 B2B and B2C marketers
- 8 top challenges to achieving success
- Sherpa's Social Marketing ROAD Map
- Budgeting and financial metrics (are you spending more than your peers?)
- Social media consumption and user behavior
- Integration of social media and email
- Integration of social media and search
- Research on Twitter, Facebook, LinkedIn and blogging

Screenshot taken from marketingsherpa.com

Marketing Sherpa sells in-depth reports on the topic of online marketing for hundreds of dollars, like the $397 report on social media shown above.

Self-publishing, publicity, online marketing, what's your specialty, and how can you use it to create a special report? It can be as simple as repurposing some material you've already written. Notice what's said about the content of the special reports found at publicityhound.com:

> Each special report, chock full of publicity tips that will help you with your public relations campaign, is at least 5 pages single-spaced. They include dozens of valuable publicity tips compiled from Joan Stewart's newsletters, workshops and consulting business. Special Reports are only available digitally. Download the reports as soon as you order and be reading them within minutes.

You, no doubt, have material that you can repurpose into a special report as well. If you have a newsletter or e-letter, you have material that could probably be transformed into a special report. You can take snippets from your training material and turn them into a special report. What do you hear yourself repeating to callers or writing in emails on a regular basis? When people repeatedly ask questions on a subject, it indicates that an interest isn't being fully addressed.

For a few weeks, keep an informal log of some sort that records the questions you get emails or calls about. You'll have the makings no doubt of several reports from that research alone. From a content delivery perspective, there's no need to get fancy. Simply write the report in a Microsoft Word document, and then convert it to a PDF so that it maintains its form and is unalterable. From Word 2007 forward you, can save a document in Word as a PDF. Or, you can buy Adobe Acrobat itself at adobeacrobat.com and create an Adobe PDF which gives you more control over the document's final output.

Determine upfront whether your audience would best be served by having a print copy option or whether you will only sell digital copies. If you choose to sell both, be sure to set a higher price for printed mailed copies.

Marketing Your Special Reports

Again, think first about how you can incorporate the sale of your special reports into what you already do. Make flyers available to walk-in traffic, put them out at exhibit tables, add them to your handouts when you give presentations, and enclose them in your usual mailings. Just as you can sell books and DVDs at speaking engagements, you can print and bind your reports and sell them as well. At Joan Stewart's site (publicityhound.com) you'll see that she bundles 52 reports for a significant savings to the buyer and a nice payday for her.

Online, your webmaster should make a new page on your site that is devoted to your reports. When you add new reports to your site, be sure to add them to the top of the page, preferably with a colorful little blinking icon that says NEW. A visit to publicityhound.com and parapublishing.com may offer page layout ideas.

If your shopping cart supports the sale of digital products, as sophisticated carts are capable of these days, you'll be selling reports in no time. A shopping cart capable of doing everything that will be mentioned throughout this book is found at kickstartcart.com.

Although you should promote each new report as it becomes available for sale in your e-letter, you should also do a special email blast announcing each new report as well. Make the subject line for such an email the topic of your report, then offer a little teaser in the body of the letter and provide a direct link to the report page. Below is an example of this format.

> **Subject:** Why Coffee Drinkers are Thinking Twice
>
> Have you ever wondered if all the recent hype about coffee drinking and aging is true? Can it be that for every cup of coffee you drink you shorten your life by an hour? If you'd like to finally get the real "scope" on coffee and you, take a look at the special report *Coffee: Morning Friend or Silent Killer?* Direct Link

The beauty of monetizing your mission with information products that come out of your work is that you already know you have an audience for them. You just need to let people know that you have the material available, and then keep them informed as you create more.

STRATEGY NUMBER 7: Produce eBooks

You no doubt have material that could easily be fleshed out into an eBook. If you have a frequently asked questions page, you have content for an eBook, one that you already know people will value because the content came from them. Your handouts from trainings you offer could be content for an eBook. What topics in your field are articles and books being written on, and interviews and speeches being given about? If you don't know, do a search at Amazon and see what pops up.

Once you have a topic in mind, you want to make sure that there's an audience for it. To do that you'll need to do a little bit of painless research. The key to writing an eBook that will sell well to the general public as well as to your stakeholders is to find the words and phrases that people are typing into search engines to find information. For example, are people typing into search engines foster care, orphanage, foster kids, or adoption when researching this subject? Which term gets the most searches?

A perfect example of this hits close to home. *Non-profit* with a dash gets 1,900 searches a day, while *non profit* with a space and no dash gets 9,000 searches a day. You would have no way of knowing this were it not for Internet tools like freekeywords.wordtracker.com, which reports daily keyword searches, or Google's keyword tool which reports monthly figures. With more than one forward slash in its site name, it's easier to find this site by simply doing a Google search on the phrase "Google keyword tool," and clicking on the first response. These tools allow you to discover the words and phrases people are typing into Google and other search engines.

You want to utilize the most popular and relevant keyword your research uncovers in your book title.

Writing the eBook

If you don't have time to sit down and write, you might try talking into a tape recorder and sending the recording out for transcription. You can find someone to transcribe your material through craigslist or by requesting a bid at a site like freelancer.com. In the latter case, it's wise to verify that it's going to be a human, not a computer, doing the work. Or, that at the very least a human will check over the work before submitting it to you. On the higher end you can look into the transcription service idictate.com. They will take your work over the telephone, or as a recorded file, or even your hand written notes. For a more personal touch there's cynrjetranscription.com. On the lower end, you can go to fiverr.com, a site where people do all sorts of things for $5, including transcribing audio files.

If you don't even have the time or energy to dictate a book and you want someone to just write the whole thing for you, you can hire a writer to do exactly that. Just go to a site like elance.com, sologig.com, writerfind.com, freelancer.com, guru.com, or odesk.com and post a job, it's completely free. Writers will respond back with a bid and the reason they believe they can handle your job.

You can specify in your post that you need a writer with expertise on the subject, or if you have the talking points and simply need someone who can run with what you have then you can specify that. You just need to put in your post what it is you're looking for.

Talking points or no, you will still need to put in some time on the book after you get it back from the writer, but the lion's share of the work will have been done for you.

Job	Budget
food related ebook writing Easy_Web_Solutio... | E-books and Blogs — Details+	$500 to $1,000
E-book Writer Needed EliteIM | E-books and Blogs — Details+	Less than $500
Complete Write Up Service For New eBook anybuys9631 | E-books and Blogs — Details+	Less than $500
Experienced eBook Writers Needed Mr.Zen | E-books and Blogs — Details+	More than $1,00
Golf instruction ebook finishing touches needed johngaltconsulti... | E-books and Blogs — Details+	Less than $500
E-book & articles on blogging & freelance writing xtrapunch | E-books and Blogs — Details+	Less than $500
Ebook required - Introduction to Options Trading marketmum | E-books and Blogs — Details+	Less than $500

Posts for eBook writers at elance.com

Hiring a Writer

When using any of the above sites to find a writer, utilize whatever the site provides to help you scrutinize the writer you're considering. For example, read their feedback, notice how long they've been registered with the site, if the site provides a rating or quality score compare theirs to others. Once you've decided on someone, give them a test project to start with so that you can assess their ability to meet deadlines, as well as the quality, speed, and accuracy of their work, and their ability to follow directions.

Most, if not all of this, can be assessed by giving the writer some specific instructions to follow for writing an article and a deadline by which to return it to you. For example, you might request the following:

> The article needs to be in a Word document, using 14 point font in Arial for the body and 24 point Arial Black for subject headings, double-spaced, margins 1.25 inches on left and right side and 0.5 inches top and bottom. Text will be justified left, ragged right. Only one space after periods. Paragraphs should not be indented. One extra space between paragraphs. Footer should have page numbers.

If someone can't take the time to get these simple instructions right, you have no reason to expect they'll follow the other instructions you'll have for completing the project.

Whenever you have someone write something for you, whether articles, special reports, or eBooks, make sure you have them sign a work-for-hire agreement to protect your interests. Your legal person can provide you with something, but it's basically a couple of paragraphs that state:

> I (writer's name) understand that the (type of work) work I do for (organization's name) is considered "Work for Hire" and that I retain no rights to or claims against this material other than the amount of money agreed upon for my salary.
>
> I also agree to create original work and I will hold (organization) harmless on any claims of plagiarism that may arise from my work.

How much might you pay to have an eBook written for you? Certainly it depends on the length of the book, but let's look at the eBooks Internet marketer Tom Antion had written for him. He put out a request for bids on Elance for two eBooks he wanted written. One was a wedding toasts eBook, and the other was a wedding speeches eBook.

In the request he also said he wanted two sales letters written. In two days he had a contract with a writer from Ohio who had been in 12 weddings in the past two years, which Tom felt clearly qualified him to write on the subject.

For both 50 page eBooks and the two sales letters, Tom paid the gentleman $550. He had to put in an additional 10 hours of his own time, which isn't bad for two 50-page books and two sales letters. And, in the end he had products he could put into the marketplace. The eBooks only retail for $17, yet over the past eight years they have generated over $175,000 each. And, they continue to generate revenue.

Technical Aspects

Just like your special reports, you write your eBook in Word and convert it to a PDF after it's finished, either by saving it as a PDF while in Word or in Adobe Acrobat. The advantage of creating an Adobe PDF in Acrobat is that if you want to you can add bookmarks, this is basically a dynamic table of contents that allows the reader to click on a chapter and jump over to it. As shown below it also allows you to password protect the material against copying and even printing if it's warranted.

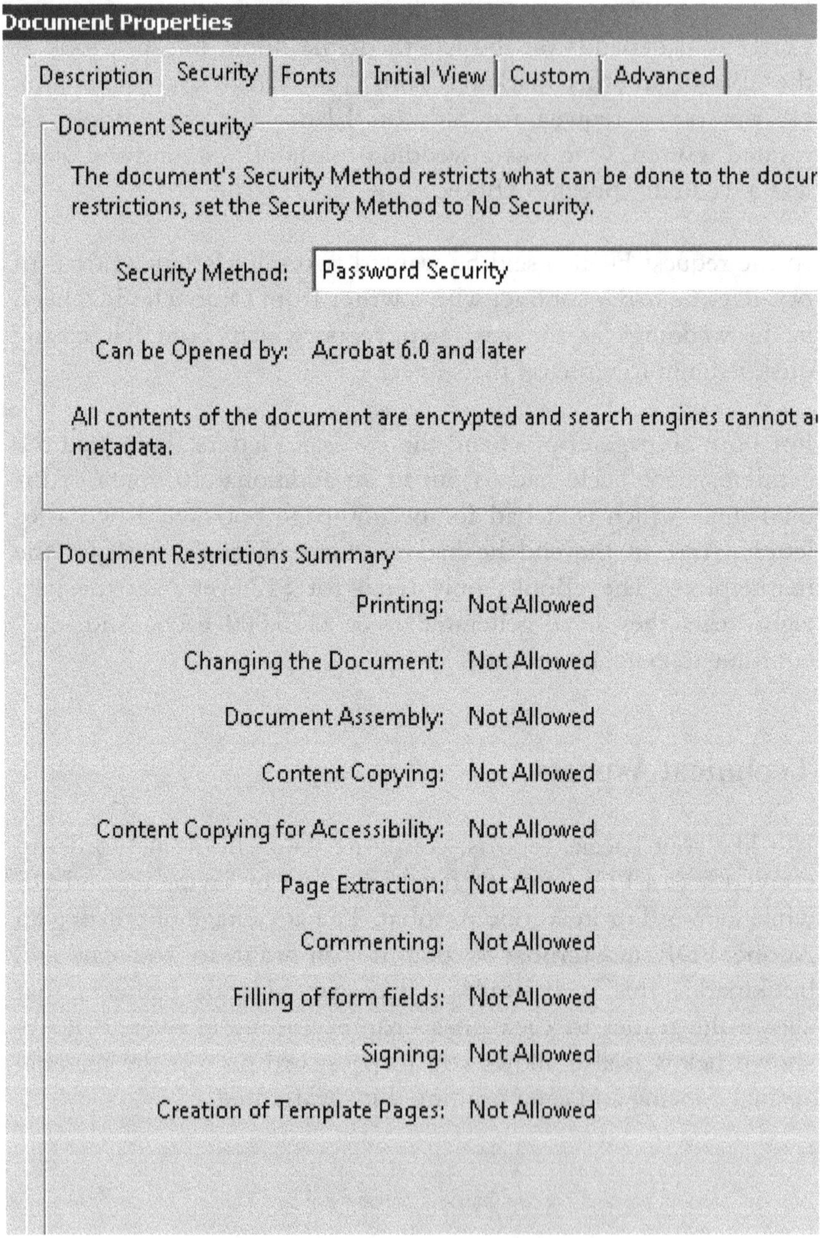

Document Properties

Description | Security | Fonts | Initial View | Custom | Advanced

Document Security

The document's Security Method restricts what can be done to the docur
restrictions, set the Security Method to No Security.

Security Method: Password Security

Can be Opened by: Acrobat 6.0 and later

All contents of the document are encrypted and search engines cannot a
metadata.

Document Restrictions Summary

Printing:	Not Allowed
Changing the Document:	Not Allowed
Document Assembly:	Not Allowed
Content Copying:	Not Allowed
Content Copying for Accessibility:	Not Allowed
Page Extraction:	Not Allowed
Commenting:	Not Allowed
Filling of form fields:	Not Allowed
Signing:	Not Allowed
Creation of Template Pages:	Not Allowed

Security setting options offered in Adobe Acrobat

So, that's the inside of the book, for the outside you should have a cover made for display on your main website. Whoever handles your graphic design needs will be able to take care of this for you. Or, if you don't have a graphics person, you can easily find someone on fiverr.com to make an eBook cover for five bucks.

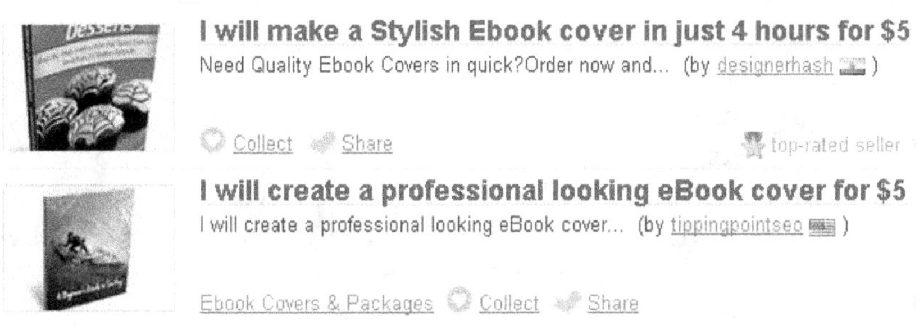

Screenshot taken from fiverr.com

To accommodate people who would prefer reading your eBook on an e-reader, you may want to have your eBook converted to a couple of the more popular e-reader formats. Smashwords is a great resource for this, at smashwords.com. They will convert your eBooks to accommodate all of the current eBook readers (except Amazon's Kindle) and distribute it at no cost. They do this in exchange for a 15 percent commission. While this is nice, it will be gravy in comparison to what you will be able to earn selling the books on your site.

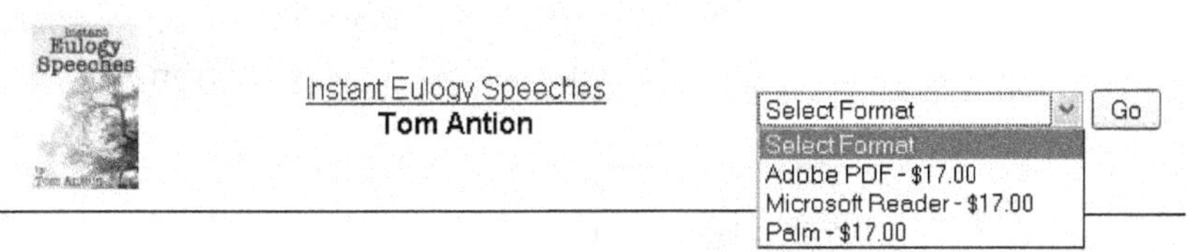

Buyers have format options

What you're really after are the free conversions they provide you with, so that you can offer your visitors a few choices, as illustrated above.

Although their conversions are free, Smashwords' formatting requirements for submitting your document are quite onerous, so depending on whether you would rather devote time or money to the project, you can alternatively find someone on sites like Elance and Odesk to do the conversion at a cost of $200 or less.

Although Amazon's Kindle is leading the charge when it comes to eBook readers, it defeats your purpose to sell your eBook on Amazon. First, you won't be able to get the buyer's information if they buy from Amazon, which means you will have no means by which to develop a relationship with them. Second, you won't generate much revenue selling eBooks on Amazon. Tom's $17 eBook would only earn him $5.95 in royalties from Amazon.

Marketing Your eBooks

To begin the discussion about marketing and selling eBooks, we need to first ask the question what's in a name? Ultimately, your eBook is a digital document. Some might call their 50 page document an eBook, while others might call it a report. Dan Poynter, who we discussed earlier, has some material on his site that he calls special reports and other material he calls documents, but you'd be hard pressed to discern the reason for the distinction. You need to give some thought to the naming of your digital products as well, asking yourself whether your stakeholders are more likely to buy an eBook, a special report, a white paper, a guide, or a document. Would they put more value on a special report or an eBook? Use the answers to these questions to name your digital products.

With that aside, let's talk about marketing the digital product we will continue to call *eBook*. Your marketing started when you did your keyword research and incorporated the most relevant and popular keyword in your book title. You're now going to use those keywords and keyword phrases in your online marketing.

Although you will list your eBook on your main site and will have a page devoted to it, it's extremely important that you have your webmaster create a website that's devoted exclusively to the sell of your eBook. Your book's keywords won't get noticed by search engines on a site filled with multiple topics, as your current site no doubt is, the way a site devoted to one subject will. This is why you want to create a simple keyword rich website dedicated to the marketing of your eBook. You should, however, provide a link from your main site to your dedicated site for search engine optimization purposes.

Keywords are like breadcrumbs that lead visitors to your site. Your domain name should incorporate a keyword, your webmaster should insert your keywords into your site's source code. And, most importantly, they must be incorporated throughout your site. If you prefer, you can find someone, as Tom Antion did, to write your sales letter(s) for you, using the sites discussed earlier: freelancer.com, elance.com, odesk.com, etc.

Google loves websites that are rich in high quality relevant content. It's the keyword usage that indicates to them that it's relevant content. They also have come to prefer sites that are longer than one page, so although you only need one page to describe your eBook, it's a good idea to add a few additional pages. Your webmaster can create a three or four page site with each page basically consisting of an advertorial for the eBook. The advertorial on the homepage should cover all of the issues surrounding the problem the eBook addresses, while the subsequent two or three pages can each be devoted to one specific issue.

Although the purpose of this dedicated site is to sell your eBook, it's important not to make it look like an ecommerce site. Never forget that people go to Google for information, they go to Amazon to shop, and they go to YouTube for tutorials.

For example, generally speaking you can bet that a person who wants to learn how to make, let's say Baklava, will go to Amazon if they want to buy a book on making it, they'll go to YouTube if they're hoping to find a video on making it, and they'll search Google if they want to download a recipe for making it. Let's look at how you can use Google and YouTube for marketing your eBook.

Google

When you create a website dedicated to your eBook, it's in the hope that it will be found in a Google search. As just discussed, once visitors find your site in Google, it's important that they feel like they've found information rather than a page trying to sell them something. So, make your homepage answer the question, or address the issue on the minds of people typing your topic into a search engine, and later down the page offer them your eBook.

Notice that there's no picture of Tom Antion's wedding speeches eBook that has done so well at wedding-speeches.org. It's fine to put the picture of your eBook cover on your main site, because people are utilizing that site for other purposes, and the eBook is just one other thing you have to offer. But, you should not have a picture of your eBook on the dedicated site. Understandably, nothing screens *SALES* to a site visitor like encountering a picture of a product.

Until you have organic traffic flowing to your dedicated site, and if the keywords associated with your topic are reasonably priced, Google's pay-per-click advertising can be an effective way to drive traffic. You can have your webmaster, or someone knowledgeable about using Google Adwords, look into creating a campaign. You might also want to research placing an ad on FaceBook, where you can use its demographic information to do a very targeted campaign.

YouTube

When optimized for search engines, YouTube videos rank very well in Google. It makes sense, therefore, to create a little two-minute screen capture video, the mechanics of which will be discussed with the next strategy, and to post it on YouTube. Again, people go to YouTube to see how to do something, not to buy something, so don't create a blatant sales video.

A two-minute video for your eBook needs to start with a hook, something like, "In this video, I'm going to show you how you may be hurting your credit without realizing it." It then needs to make two or three good points utilizing a visual. And it's best to end it by incentivizing people to visit your site. For example, "To receive a free copy of *Better Credit in 90 Days* visit credithelp.com."

Example of a watermark on a video

The software for making screen capture videos allows you to insert a watermark, and you should do this. A watermark is something that shows the entire time your video is playing. You should use this watermark at the bottom of your video to either display your website, or preferably, your incentive: **For a FREE copy of *Better Credit in 90 Days* visit CreditHelp.com.**

To follow are the steps you need to take to get your video picked up by Google. Use freekeywords.wordtracker.com, or Google's keyword tool, to create a list of the keywords associated with your eBook's subject. Create your video's title, its description, and its tags (another word for keywords) with search engines in mind.

Video titles are searchable, so the first word of your video's title should be the most important keyword from your list. Be sure to also use keywords in your video's description. Be sure to include your incentive and your website address in the description box as well. As always, the digital product you're using as an incentive should be tied in with an opt-in box, as discussed earlier. In the space provided for tags, enter the rest of the keywords from your list, as well as common misspellings. There's no need to repeat the keywords you used in the title and description.

When uploading your video you'll have some decisions to make, like do you want people to be able to comment on your video or not. If you want to keep life simple, it's best not to allow it. But it's a good idea to turn on ratings, since search engines like videos that have high ratings.

Unless your topic is associated with very competitive keywords, if you follow these steps for posting your video on YouTube you should show up in Google, MSN, and Yahoo pretty quickly, which means you'll have traffic going to your site. When that happens, rename your video and repost it. Also, post it on your organization's Facebook page if you have one. You can also submit your video to the other popular sites for video as well: yahoo.com, myspace.com, dailymotion.com, metacafe.com, revver.com, viddler.com, and crackle.com.

Revenue Share

Another marketing strategy for moving your eBooks is to ask organizations whose people are your people, whether private sector or public, to display a link on their site to your dedicated eBook site. Some organizations might be willing to display a link without a revenue split, but for others you can offer to set them up as an affiliate, whereby they earn a referral commission of your choosing when someone buys the eBook as a result of that affiliation.

A sophisticated shopping cart system makes it simple to set up such an affiliate program, it provides a unique link to your site for each affiliate. When someone visits your site via that link and buys your eBook, that purchase is attributed to the affiliate associated with the link. This should sound familiar from the discussion on affiliate marketing, except this time the roles are reversed, you're the merchant with the product. The shopping cart keeps track of all the commissions due each one of your affiliates, all you have to do is cut affiliate checks at the end of the month. Using affiliates to promote your eBook can dramatically increase your eBook's exposure and sales.

One place to look for affiliates is associations. If there is an association out there that aligns with your organization's mission, it makes sense for you to know about them and for their people to know about you. They could, in fact, be a target audience for some of the strategies we're discussing.

Your library probably has a reference copy of *National Trade and Professional Associations of the United States*, as well as the *State and Regional Associations of the United States.* These guides list over 7,000 associations and labor unions, providing you with an easy way to discover organizations across the country.

STRATEGY NUMBER 8: Produce Instructional CDs or DVDs

Creating an instructional CD involves many of the same steps discussed in creating a CD of stories, except that in this case you, or a staff member, or a volunteer, or someone you've hired, will stand in front of a microphone and instruct. For a DVD, you will need to hire a videographer and editor as discussed earlier. Since you'll be instructing, you will no doubt also need a teleprompter to scroll your presentation in front of you. Tell your videographer you need a teleprompter technician, you will simply need to provide the tech with your finished script. This could cost $200-400 for the day. If you would like to practice reading from a scrolling screen, you can download the teleprompter software known as Prompt! at movieclip.biz/prompt.html.

If your presentation involves something that can be shown on your computer, let's say demonstrating how to respond to a request for proposal (RFP), then rather than a videographer you simply need screen capture software. Screen capture programs allow you to record anything you can display on your computer screen, whether it's something online or a PowerPoint presentation, if you can see it on your computer you can capture and record it. You simply need to plug in your USB microphone, as we talked about before, and narrate. You edit your recording right there within the program as well. You just highlight and cut out segments you don't want. There's no pressure to be perfect because you can just record snippets, edit them, and then string them all together.

When you're finished editing, the program walks you through the clicking of a few buttons that let's the software render your recording as a DVD. When it's done you have a DVD master that can be duplicated. Whether you need to make YouTube videos or professional training videos, screen capture software makes the task very simple, and offers high quality results.

Camtasia is a popular screen capture program that is very easy to use, and it comes with explicit video tutorials. You can get the latest version of Camtasia, and even download a 30 day free trial, by going to their site. Camtasia is a TechSmith product, so you can find it either at techsmith.com, or camtasia.com. It costs just under $300 for PC, and just under $100 for Mac. A free utility that allows you to play around with screen capture can be found at camstudio.org.

Let's Back Up

Let me just state what you've known for a long time, but which has special meaning when you start using your computer for creating information products as we've been discussing. And that is to back up your work on a separate data holder. Don't make the mistake of thinking you'll start backing up your work when you go down and buy a fancy super synched up external gizmo with all of the bells and whistles. That's like not getting any car insurance until you can afford full coverage. Insure your work by backing it up on whatever you have right now, a memory stick, a writeable DVD, take something, and take it regularly, and back up your work. An internal back up is useless if your whole computer seizes up on you or your drive gets damaged, because you won't be able to access the back up.

The best approach is the triple threat, you have it on your hard drive and on two other sources. Carbonite, at carbonite.com, for a nominal yearly fee, serves as a good automated backup option that requires no hardware. Once installed, it automatically backs up new files on your computer; it encrypts the information and stores it on Carbonite's server. Whenever you need to, you can get on any computer and go to their site; enter your password and gain access to your files.

Packaging and Shipping

So, now you have this DVD or CD and you want to package it nicely; after all, it will be commercially priced. Although music CDs tend to be packaged in plastic jewel cases, they're made of hard plastic that crack easily. They also don't offer much in the way of a substantial look for an instructional program. DVD cases, on the other hand, look more like a 6 x 9 book (see left picture below), and they're made of a more durable material. If your program has multiple discs you can use a DVD or CD album. Some albums hold discs on one side and they have a literature hub on the opposing side for placing material, as shown below. Blackbourn is a company that sells this kind of packaging (blackbourn.com). You can reach them at (800) 842-7550.

Photos compliments of blackbourn.com

When it comes to shipping supplies, Uline has a 400 page catalog filled with every shipping product imaginable. They're at uline.com, or 800-295-5510. You can order from them 24 hours a day, and they offer same day shipping. Their prices are extremely competitive.

Whether you're shipping DVDs, CDs, books or other items, it can be useful to get a volunteer to come in to do some prepackaging so that when an order comes in all that needs to be done is to finalize it and ship it out. If you don't currently do a lot of shipping, you should compare the price of the postal service's flat rate boxes with UPS and FedEx ground to determine the best way to ship your products.

If you believe volunteers won't make your life easy enough, you can utilize the services of a fulfillment company. They will do everything for you. You supply them with your merchandise, and have your shopping cart send an order notification email to them in addition to yourself. When an order comes in, it's emailed to them as well as to you, and you don't have to do a thing.

You're going to pay between $2 to $4 a package for this service, but if the profit margin allows for it it's one way to take all order fulfillment off of your hands. Some fulfillment houses will also duplicate your material on demand for an extra fee, in addition to shipping it.

Two fulfillment companies you can look into include Speaker Fulfillment Services, Inc (speakerfulfillmentservices.com) at 812-877-7100, and McMannis Duplication (mcmannisduplication.com) at 620-628-4411. You can also Google "fulfillment companies" to see what you find.

Marketing

Before you implement this strategy you must know who your target audience is, and what your price point will be. The key is to consider the individuals, organizations, institutions, agencies, businesses, or associations that need this information. Once you determine who needs the information and what your price point is, you will know the kind of marketing you can afford to do.

Having an easily defined target audience means you should be able to obtain a mailing list for your group and do a brochure mailing, if your product has a high enough price point. You can obtain a mailing list for just about any group of people imaginable by working with the appropriate list broker. All list brokers, however, are not created equal. Some keep their lists fresh and updated, and they really care about quality and retaining customers. Others, in a word, don't. MCH keeps good lists. They're at mchdata.com. Their niche is institutions, but they're a good resource for brokers of lists they don't carry themselves.

Let your website market for you as well. Have a page made that does a good job of describing your instructional program. Take a few snippets from your DVD program that you feel provide a good sense of it, and have your webmaster put it up on your website. For CDs, let visitors to your site hear a sample of it. A webpage worth modeling is antion.com/imcds.htm. With a click of one button visitors can listen to a sample of the CD that's for sale, and with the click on an accompanying link they're taken to a full sales letter page devoted to that title. This is a site that's worth looking at and learning from.

One of the easiest ways to put sound on your site, which includes providing a sample of your CD, is through the service of AudioGenerator (audiogenerator.com). In fact, this is the service in use on the site just mentioned. The service has a monthly fee, but it makes putting audio on your website very simple.

If you can't think of a topic for this strategy, solicit suggestions. Surveymonkey.com makes sending surveys very easy. Send out a survey to agencies, stakeholders, appropriate nonprofits, individuals who subscribe to your e-letter, donors, whoever makes the most sense, and ask them questions. You might be surprised by what you discover.

STRATEGY NUMBER 9: Host a Contest

This strategy requires thinking of a form of expression, whether short story, photo, essay, video, artwork, song, spoken word, or something else, and choosing a topic. The topic could be the cause your organization is focused on. An organization whose cause is helping emancipated foster care youth, for example, might hold a photo contest on the subject *Life after Aging Out.*

Entrants have a chance to express what the topic means to them using the prescribed format. You decide on how many places beyond a winner you will have, and whether you might have honorable mentions. You can recruit a committee of volunteers to serve as judges. And, of course, what's a contest without prizes? These will, naturally, come through in-kind donations. There are so many possibilities when it comes to prizes.

You will also have to determine the fees associated with entering the contest. To follow are some of the more well known contests and their fees. Communication Arts Photography Competition (commarts.com/competitions/photography) charges $35 for a single entry and $70 for a series. Pictures of the Year International (poyi.org) charges $50 per entry, PDN (pdnphotoannual.com) charges $45 for single and $55 for series.

For the written word, Dayton Literary Peace Prize (daytonliterarypeaceprize.org) charges $100 per entry for works of fiction and nonfiction that foster peace, social justice, and global understanding. The Story Prize (thestoryprize.org) is an annual book award honoring the author of an outstanding collection of short fiction, they charge a $75 entry fee for each book.

Tiered entry fees are also common, they consist of an entry fee for meeting the initial deadline and two higher fees for two subsequent deadlines. Once you decide on the form of expression your contest will utilize, do an online search for that type of contest and snoop around. But in the long run, this will be your contest that you will make unique to your organization.

You decide on your guidelines, for example, a word length for an essay or short story contest, whether you will impose a maximum number of entries per person, or if you will specify a video or song length? These are creative questions that hopefully you'll have fun entertaining.

You will also need to come up with participation rules. Take a look at the rules for a few contests and in no time your rules should take shape. Here are some ideas:

> All entry fees are non-refundable.
>
> All (works) entered become the physical property of (organization) and will not be returned.
>
> (Organization) is not responsible for late, lost, damaged, misdirected, postage due, stolen, incomplete, or misappropriated entries.
>
> All entries submitted must be original (works) and shall not infringe on any copyrights or any other rights of any third parties.
>
> Entrant agrees that should his/her (works) be selected as a winner, (organization) shall have the right to use the winning (works) for promotional purposes.

To view examples of contest rules, you can visit songwritingcompetition.com, or independentpublisher.com, as well as the other sites listed above. Your legal person will no doubt have some suggestions as well.

Marketing Your Contest

Throwing a contest is like throwing a party, it takes people for it to be successful. Although you know how to reach your people, for a contest you need to reach far beyond your people. Be sure to set deadlines your first year that will allow you enough time to promote it and get a good response.

Have a few volunteers generate buzz through social networking sites. Of course, you'll dedicate a page to the contest on your website. Do an email blast about it to all of your stakeholders. Have postcards made up and enlist a group of volunteers to leave stacks in establishments that get a lot of foot traffic. Enlist the help of volunteers from all across the country. They should be sure to replenish the stacks as needed.

Reach out to the media, your local paper should definitely write a piece about your organization's *first annual contest.* Radio should help you out as well. You want to always market your contest with a global reach in mind, but initially your biggest draw will no doubt be from your local area.

The following year, and each year thereafter, your numbers will grow as new people learn of the contest and as you email your prior year's entrants. Over time, your organization will become known for its contest, and you will experience the momentum that comes from having a reputation. Imagine the awareness this will raise for your cause and organization.

You stand to have a lot of fun with this strategy in addition to generating a healthy revenue stream.

STRATEGY NUMBER 10: Host Webinars and Teleseminars

Teleseminars and webinars are a very convenient way of holding a class on a topic of interest to your stakeholders. If you haven't already done so, it's a good idea to start thinking about subjects. If you're unclear about this, you can simply administer a survey. Inform survey takers that you plan on scheduling a number of classes throughout the year and that you want to make sure the classes are on topics that they care about. Armed with a list of subjects you now have a decision to make.

There are two types of teleseminars/webinars—paid and promotional. You need to decide which type you will offer. Promotional teleseminars/webinars are free to attend because they're designed around selling a product, service, or an event, and the revenue is generated from those sales. It's best to decide upfront which type you will offer so that people will come to expect that from you. If you offer primarily free classes interspersed with paid ones, you may find people passing on those that cost because they know a free one is around the corner. If, on the other hand, you only offer paid classes your followers will learn that access comes at a price.

For paid classes you will, naturally, need to decide on a price. You may want to charge less for teleseminars, for example $29.95, than webinars for which you might charge $39.95 or $49.95. These are common middle of the road prices, although there are higher priced classes as well. Once you choose a price, keep it. Don't charge $39.95 for some webinars and $49.95 for others. When the time comes to increase the price do it, but until that time be consistent.

Webinars vs. Teleseminars

Webinars have really picked up where teleseminars left off, but offering what makes the most sense for you and your people is the most important consideration. Interacting with your attendees completely by telephone, teleseminars are not very conducive to demonstrations. You can, however, provide attendees with a link to a PDF handout, so there is an opportunity to provide some visuals.

When it comes to cost and equipment for teleseminars, it makes the most sense to start off by using a free service like freeconferencecall.com. Most free services restrict the number of attendees to under 100. Their paid plans accommodate numbers far beyond that.

Webinars offer a chance to demonstrate, in addition to instruct, because they allow participants to see your computer screen. This means you can provide a training, demonstrate the steps of a process, illustrate real time usage of a software or website. Sadly, in the public sector webinars often consist of a PowerPoint presentation where the person is just reading what's on the screen. Such a boring presentation won't suffice for paid webinars. If this is the type of content you have to offer, it would make more sense to hold a teleseminar with a handout that has your talking points. This is better than blatantly reading to your audience.

As far as cost and equipment for webinars are concerned, a commonly used service for webinars is GoToWebinar found at gotowebinar.com. Unlike teleseminar companies, they do not have a free option. Instead, they have monthly plans that vary in cost based on the number of attendees. Webinars are definitely more to manage technically than a teleseminar, especially if you're fielding questions as you go; having a sidekick can simplify things. GoToWebinar requires that attendees download software, and if they don't have Java Script enabled on their computer they can experience problems getting the program to load. If they do have Java Script installed and enabled, then the software downloads and the program launches in seconds without requiring any user effort. Although Adobe has a webinar program that doesn't require downloading software, it doesn't compare favorably to GotoWebinar at this time.

Recording

Most services allow you to record your teleseminars and webinars, although recording it yourself as a backup is a good idea as well, just in case there's a glitch of some kind. There are two very important reasons for securing a recording, (1) it allows you to encourage people to sign up even if they're not 100 percent certain that they'll be able to attend the live session, because they'll have access to the teleseminar's recording, or the webinar's replay, and (2) your recording or replay becomes a new information product that you can sell for the price you charged to attend the live class. Be sure to charge the same price for them as for the live event or people are sure to realize that they'll save money by buying them rather than attending live.

Content for Paid Versus Free Classes

The content you will provide in a class varies depending on whether it is a paid or a free promotional class. Free classes offer rich content but they do not offer detailed step-by-step instructions. They provide steps on why you need to do something, or what it is you need to do, but they don't provide steps for how to do it. Or, if they do provide the how, it's to demonstrate how much the task entails, setting the stage for the product or service for sale at the end of the class that simplifies the process.

Let's consider a webinar titled *What's at the Root of Donation Drop Offs*, as an example. On a paid webinar, attendees would be told the causes for donation drop offs, followed by the steps to take to prevent drop offs from occurring, as well as tips for what to do if they've already experienced a drop off. A free webinar, on the other hand, would simply focus on the root cause of donation drop offs, in keeping with the title of the webinar. After explaining what causes drop offs, attendees would be given a chance to purchase an information product that explains what to do about drop offs if they've already occurred, and how to prevent them if they haven't. This is the format a free promotional webinar takes. If you get the mix right, always delivering on the promised title, while offering a spot on continuing education product, you will have happy attendees who will come to value your classes.

Webinars and teleseminars are a great place for you to sell your intellectual property. On a webinar you can have a slide that shows the webpage that has your product offer, and you can also put the live link into the chat box so attendees can simply click on it and be taken to your offer page. If you haven't attended many webinars in the private sector it would be wise to view or attend both paid and free promotional classes so you can get a feel for them. For examples of paid webinars you can visit publicityhound.com, and for examples of free promotional classes visit tomantionwebinars.com.

Joint Ventures

In addition to promoting your own material, you can also do a joint venture with someone who has a product or service you believe would be beneficial to your people. It might be a coaching program or a seminar, it might be a physical product that one of your vendors sells. Joint ventures are best formed over big ticket items, although that doesn't have to be the case. A special webpage is set up for attendees to take advantage of the offer. Naturally, you decide on the arrangement in advance, but a 50/50 split is common.

Your guest makes a special offer for those on the call or webinar. It should be a generous enticing package at a good price for your people. Don't be afraid to ask for an additional goodie or a better discount if you feel the package is not sweet enough. After all, you hold the cards, you have the people. It's not a bad idea to also incentivize taking immediate action by offering an extra bonus of some kind. This could be 30 minutes of free consulting time with your guest to the first 20 people who take action. On the recording, be sure to delete references to any incentives that aren't applicable after the live call has ended.

Joint ventures offer a nice income potential with little effort on the part of the host. For example, your 50 percent of a $700 program sold to just 35 attendees would generate over $12,000 for your organization. And, all you had to do was promote the event to your people and host the class. By sending out an email with the replay link, being clear that the replay will come down in 72 hours, you will pick up some additional sales.

On these kinds of webinars, you will only need to welcome your attendees, let them know how excited you are to have the day's guest, read your guest's introduction, and turn over the reigns. You can monitor the chat box for comments and questions during the presentation.

Joint ventures are a definite win-win-win—your people win as they gain valuable information and an opportunity to invest further in their needs or education. You win as you generate revenue, and your joint venture partner wins by gaining an audience and sharing in the revenue. When you come across physical products, information products, seminars, home study courses, coaching or consulting programs that you feel would benefit your people, why not reach out to the creator of those items and discuss a joint venture opportunity.

Upsells

In addition to the money you will earn selling attendance to the teleseminars or webinars themselves, you can boost your earnings by offering a related digital product during the signup process. Known as an upsell, this is a very simple but effective technique that McDonalds popularized back in the day with the offer, "want fries with that?" Fast food aside, this is how it works in the online world. After someone pays to attend your teleseminar/webinar, a page appears that offers them a chance to purchase a related product. If they click *Yes* the item is automatically added to their order, without them having to reenter their credit card information. If they click *No* they're directed to a thank you page for having signed up for the event. Alternatively, you can bundle the offer in the shopping cart where a person can choose to add it during check out, as demonstrated below.

Quantity	Product	Price	Total	Remove
1	**Webinar--35 Ways to Promote Your Facebook Page**	$49.95	$49.95	X
0	**How to Use Pinterest-Bonus offer** Pinterest, the hot social media site that's growing faster than Fastbook and Google+, isn't just for pretty pictures of wedding dresses and cupcakes.	$24.97	$0.00	X

An upsell displayed in the shopping cart

It makes perfect sense really. If I'm signing up for your $49.95 webinar on *Parenting in the World of the Wired*, and you offer me instant access to the recording of a teleseminar with a parenting expert, normally priced at $39.95 discounted to $24.95, I'm pretty inclined to snap it up. Some Internet marketers find that 30-50 percent of their attendees purchase their upsell. Upsells are so easy to set up and so effective that it makes no sense not to use them.

Marketing Teleseminars and Webinars

You will want to advertise your classes on your website. You may want to visit Joan Stewart's site at publicityhound.com, she holds paid webinars regularly and you will be able to see how she has incorporated them into her site.

If you have an email list that's appropriate for the subject of your webinar or teleseminar, emailing your list is one of the fastest ways to fill it. Again, this is one of the advantages of offering visitors to your website a free digital product in exchange for their email address.

Your email invitation to attend your teleseminars and webinars needs to entice readers to click on the included link that will take them to a sales page like the one for the Facebook webinar shown below.

Thursdays are a good day to hold a class because it allows you to begin the invitation process on a Sunday. To ensure a good turn out, you will need to send out four or five additional invitations. You will also need to send out reminders. On the pages to follow are examples and templates for these kinds of emails.

12 More Ways to Avoid Missed Opportunities on the New & Improved Facebook

Time: 4 to 5:15 p.m. Eastern Time on Tuesday, March 15

Your Presenters:

Joan Stewart
The Publicity Hound
Christine Buffaloe
Serenity Virtual
Assistant Services

Registration: $49.95 (includes bonuses)

Overview:

If you're confused or frustrated by all the new changes to FaceBook, this is the webinar for you! Joan and Chris will walk you through what's new and show you how to make FaceBook really work for you to attract followers and fans, share your best content and really promote your expertise.

Who Should Attend:

- FaceBook newbies
- Anyone who has been on FaceBook awhile but is confused by how to use the new features
- FaceBook page administrators
- Anyone who is on FaceBook but doesn't know how to use a fan page
- Virtual assistants who manage their clients' FaceBook accounts
- Publicists and PR pros who want to show their clients how to incorporate FaceBook into a publicity campaign
- Anyone who needs to connect with influential people in their own industry or targeted industries

Taken from publicityhound.com

SAMPLE: Initial Invitation

Dear Sally, (first name is auto-generated)

Don't miss this chance to learn from an expert how to know if your child is using drugs.

On Thursday October 12th at 6:00 p.m. Pacific Time I will be interviewing renowned parenting coach and noted author Jane Doe on the warning signs of drug use in our children. You won't want to miss this.

Even if your schedule prevents you from joining us live, the first 100 to register get a complimentary CD of the call and I'll pay the shipping (for teleseminars), your registration gains you access to the replay (for webinars).

If you know how to do it, determining whether your child is using or is at risk of using drugs can be very painless for all involved.

In this (teleseminar/webinar) we'll be discussing the exact steps to take to discover if your child is currently using drugs, has ever used drugs, or is at risk of becoming a drug user.

You Will Learn:

=> The five red flags of drug use that many parents miss because they don't know them when they see them.

=> What your child's class schedule can tell you.

=> What innocent actions could be putting your child at risk of later deciding to use drugs.

=> The mistake most parents make when trying to determine if their children are experimenting, and how to avoid it.

=> How to broach the conversation of drug use with your child, and at what age the conversation should take place.

=> How to respect your child's privacy while not burying your head in the sand.

And much, much more.

==============

Be one of the first 100 to register and get the complimentary CD.

www.KidsandDrugs.com/teleseminars.htm

==============

Sign up now!

I'll talk to you Thursday night.
Pam Hogan
222-222-2222

P.S. Don't forget — telephone bridge line space is limited and this teleclass is sure to sell out quickly. Visit www.KidsandDrugs.com/teleseminars.htm now before all the complimentary CDs are gone. And don't forget the shipping is on me.

Or:

P.S. Visit www.KidsandDrugs.com/webinars now while there's still space available to ensure access to the class and the replay.

Kids and Drugs
PO Box 2222
Mytown, CA 94111

TEMPLATE: Initial Invitation

Here are three ways you might construct your opening paragraph:

1. Use the title of the class:
"How to Respond to RFPs With Winning Proposals NOW"

> This (teleseminar/webinar) is guaranteed to teach you how to construct a proposal designed to win government contracts worth thousands of dollars, whether you've never responded to an RFP or you have years of experience.

2. Ask a Question:
Do you have 70 minutes to spare this Thursday, October 12th?

> I hope the answer is YES, because that's when I'll be hosting a (teleseminar/webinar) that will show you how to get by on a shrinking budget with minimum staff in a bad economy.

3. Make a Statement:
Don't miss this chance to learn from an expert how to know if your child is using drugs.

> On Thursday October 12th at 6:00 p.m. Pacific Time I will be interviewing renowned parenting coach and noted author Jane Doe on the warning signs of drug use in our children. You won't want to miss this.

To follow are suggestions for constructing the body of the email.

State the importance of the information:

If you know how to do it, __(topic)__ can __(result)__ .

If you know how to do it, <u>responding to RFPs</u> can <u>be extremely lucrative.</u>

Tell them why they should attend:

In this (teleseminar/webinar) I'll be showing you the exact steps to take to ________________.

In this webinar I'll be showing you the exact steps to take to discover if your child is currently using drugs, has ever used drugs, or is at risk of becoming a drug user.

Use bullets to highlight what will be covered:

You will learn:
=>
=>
=>
=>
=>
=>
=>

As with all online sales, after a person has purchased a seat in your webinar/teleseminar, they will be directed to a thank you page. For your buyer's convenience, you should also send them a confirmation email that they can hold on to.

For a teleseminar, this email will contain the correct phone number and the pin number attendees will need to use to access the call. For webinars, the webinar company will email your buyer with those particulars; however, you will still want to send a confirmation email. Your confirmation letter and thank you page can be the same.

SAMPLE: Confirmation Email/Thank You Page

Dear Frank,

You made a great decision signing up for Pam's training "How to Respond to RFPs With Winning Proposals NOW."

Teleseminar: If you can't make it, the CD will be shipped to you after the recording is edited, duplicated and packaged. You'll also get an email with the MP3 recording the day after the class.

Webinar: If you can't make it, you'll get an email with a link to the replay.

On Thursday evening October 12th the call will start at
6:00 PM Pacific Time
7:00 PM Mountain Time
8:00 PM Central Time
9:00 PM Eastern Time

Teleseminar: Phone Number to dial 222-222-2222.
Your PIN for Thursday October 12th is 260987#

We will start promptly at 6:00 p.m. PST.

Here's a tool to help you determine your time zone: timeanddate.com/worldclock

Want more information on responding to RFPs? Check out our training room at our membership site www.RFPsMadeSimple.com

We look forward to having you on the call,
Beverly
Client Support
Save the Whales
650-888-8888
Recipient of over $500,000 in government grants

Reminders

It's critical that you remind those registered for the class to attend, and that you provide the class information again as a convenience.

Below is a sample reminder email.

Hi Jan,

Just a reminder for you that you've signed up for today's teleclass "How to Respond to RFPs With Winning Proposals NOW" at 6:00 PM Pacific Time and to make sure you have the dial-in numbers handy to join us.

You won't want to miss participating in today's call where you'll be learning how to make sure you know exactly what goes into a winning proposal.

(Insert call in details and instructions)

We look forward to having you on the call.

Beverly
Client Support
Save the Whales
650-888-8888
Recipient of over $500,000 in government grants

Additional Invitations

As previously stated, you will not get the attendance you need by only sending one invitation to your list. You will need to send four or five additional invitations. You simply need to come up with a new subject line and introductory sentence, but the body of the email can be taken from the original invitation. Below are examples of how you might introduce subsequent invitations.

Assuming the initial invitation went out on a Sunday, to follow are five additional invitations.

Monday Invitation:

Subject: Did You Get My Email Yesterday?

I just want to follow up on yesterday's email about my upcoming teleseminar/webinar on Thursday October 12th. You won't want to miss this.

(*Insert the body from the original email.*)

Tuesday Invitation:

Subject: Should we expect you?

Have you registered yet? *(link to registration page)*

I hope you know I wouldn't take the time to email you again if I wasn't 100% sure that this is a teleseminar/webinar you won't want to miss.

(*Insert the body from the original email.*)

Wednesday Invitation:

Subject: Did you forget?

I hope you get this in time, because tomorrow I'm hosting a teleseminar/webinar that you won't want to miss.

(*Insert the body from the original email.*)

Thursday (Morning):

Subject: Today's the Day—My Powerful Teleseminar Tells All

Dear Sue:

(*Insert the body from the original email.*)

Thursday (Two Hours Before Event):

Subject: Last Chance—Don't Miss It

Dear Sue:

(*Insert the body from the original email.*)

All of these additional invitations and reminders are set up in advance in your shopping cart or email marketing program as sequential autoresponders. They're programmed to be sent on the days you designate, with the number 0 representing immediately, etc. This prevents you from having to worry about sending any of them yourself. Even if you're a technophobe, you can schedule sequential autoresponders. Sending so many additional invitations may seem excessive, but it's what it takes to ensure a good turn out.

Taking Questions

If you don't want to take questions on a teleseminar, you can say something like this in the confirmation email, "With such a large crowd Pam won't be able to field questions during the class, so email them to the office either before or after the seminar and she'll do her best to get back to you with an answer as soon as she can (expect it to be at least a couple of days)."

If you do want to take questions during the call, when you begin the call mention, "With such a large crowd I won't be able to stop and take questions during the call so write them down and stay until after the main seminar and I'll answer them then." For the sake of the recording, officially end the call prior to taking the calls, "Well that brings this call to an end, thanks so much for attending. Now for those of you still on the line who have any questions I'll be happy to take them now." Unmute the call to open the lines for questions. If it's too chaotic to make anything out, look at the area codes of the callers and specify an area you want to hear from: "Okay, I only want those of you from the 415 or 408 area code with a question to speak up." And, continue in this way until it's less chaotic.

For webinars, you can have attendees write their questions into the chat box provided by the webinar company for audience participation, and you can either field them during or after the presentation. This is where a sidekick can come in handy.

With a little practice, holding these kinds of classes should become second nature. It would be a good idea, however, to hold a couple of practice sessions with staff, to get comfortable with it before holding your first one.

STRATEGY NUMBER 11: Hold Workshops

Holding workshops involves knowing who your people are, and developing a workshop around a subject of interest to those people. Once you know your people, and you have an appropriate topic, marketing becomes simple. After all, as discussed in the previous section, you don't need hundreds of people to attend your workshops for them to be successful. In fact, with the right price point, a mere 25-30 people in attendance can generate a healthy revenue stream.

Finding Your Topic and Audience

First and foremost, don't be afraid to think broadly when it comes to topics, and don't forget to look right under your nose. For example, have you come to take for granted the skills involved in juggling the number of clients your organization serves with a limited staff? There are managers out there who could no doubt benefit from your workshop on *Time Management For Understaffed Managers—Making Every Minute Count.*

Now, just in case you're feeling hesitation along the lines of, *who am I to offer a workshop?* Take a look at the national training companies, such as Fred Pryor and SkillPath Seminars. These companies hire people just like you, people whose background has made them familiar with a subject matter. Some of these companies only ask that a person have three years relevant experience in the topic area, they hand them a curriculum and they're off. So, please don't allow yourself to get hung up on not feeling qualified to hold a workshop, you are the gene pool from which these national companies pull.

It's important, however, to safeguard against relying too heavily on one person's expertise for workshop development and delivery. You don't want to look around one day and realize that you built an income stream around one individual's knowledge base, and when that person leaves the organization so does the ability to offer workshops. To prevent this from happening record the class once a quarter. This doesn't have to involve fancy equipment, just a good quality digital recorder is all that's needed. You will then be able to transfer the recording to your computer. Once a year you should have the recording transcribed. By following these simple steps your training will always be at the ready for the organization as a whole.

In the process of teaching any workshop, what tends to happen is your class participants will ask questions that go beyond the scope of your topic or time constraints. Allow these questions to alert you to new workshop topics that you can develop. Also, consider how these questions might be addressed in a manual or quick start guide that you can offer for sell at your workshops.

Now you may be saying, but our clients wouldn't be an appropriate target audience for a workshop. Fortunately, your workshops don't necessarily have to be marketed to your clients. If you open the lens up a bit you will find your people. This is what you should be asking yourself:

- Who else cares about or works with this population?
- Who would benefit from learning how to work effectively with this group?
- Who would benefit from a topic related to this population?

Here is an example of how to find your audience when you can't market to your clients. We'll take three groups that admittedly would not be a proper target for paid workshops: at-risk youth, individuals who are homeless, and pregnant teens. We'll start with at-risk youth and consider who else cares about or works with at-risk youth? Who would benefit from learning how to work effectively with at-risk youth? Who would benefit from a topic related to at-risk youth? One resounding answer is new teachers in high risk school districts.

Once you know your group, you want to ask can I reach this group? For teachers in high risk school districts the answer is *yes.* The next question you need to ask is, if I were to get just one percent of this group to attend a workshop would I be able to hit my target number of 25-30 attendees? In this scenario, that means you would need to ask yourself if there are at least 3,000 teachers working in high risk school districts in driving distance from our location (to keep things at their simplest). If so, you could promote a workshop to them that addresses their challenges: **We will use our agency experience of helping 2,000 at-risk youth a year to help you learn in one short day what it painfully takes some teachers years to learn.** Why on earth wouldn't a new teacher still learning the ropes attend your workshop?

Who would benefit from learning how to work effectively with individuals who are homeless? What about groups that offer job readiness programs, or any group looking to extend their services to this population for the first time but don't know how to reach them? Both groups would benefit from the workshop titled, *Reaching the Homeless Population: A Workshop for Service Providers.*

Who cares about or works with pregnant teens? Parents of teens who are not pregnant and who would like to keep it that way. A workshop for parents titled ***How to Talk to Your Kids about Sex, Drugs, and Pregnancy*** coming from an organization that has come to understand what teens need to hear, after having heard it all themselves, would no doubt appeal to a lot of parents. By entertaining these simple three questions it shouldn't be hard to think of groups to market workshops to if your clients, or stakeholders in general, aren't your target audience.

You should also think beyond topics directly linked to the population you serve. One workshop topic that is quite valuable and one that you may underestimate is your knowledge around effectively responding to RFPs. There are so many people struggling over responding to their first RFP, or trying to get that first award who could benefit from a workshop on this topic. Proposal readers comment about how often people miss out on funding because they simply don't do what the RFP asks. This demonstrates that people need help just understanding an RFP. If you have this skill, this is definitely a workshop subject worth considering: **Learn from an organization that has been awarded over $200,000 in grants and discover how you can do the same.** So as not to teach your skills to your competition, a training of this kind would best be offered to private sector companies with government contract opportunities—landscapers, janitors, trades people, printers, and the like.

When choosing a topic for businesses, make sure it's one where its affect on the bottom line is obvious. It's important to look at the subject critically and to ask, will it help their people make more widgets, or make widgets faster? Will it prevent the company from losing money? Helping their people so that they'll do a better job of serving the company is the business most companies are in, not helping for the sake of helping. So, don't make the mistake of carving out a workshop on a topic like transcendental meditation believing it will appeal to a manager if you can't provide evidence that it reduces absenteeism, or the like.

Pricing Workshops

There is quite a disparity when it comes to the price of workshops in the marketplace. Some workshops cost $10,000 and more to attend, while others are in the $2400 range, and you have the national training companies that charge only $199. What accounts for these differences?

If we start with workshops commanding five figures, it's important to remember that such a price didn't get set overnight. As the workshop grew in popularity so did the price tag. It's much like music talent, no one starts out pricing their concert tickets at $500 a seat, nor do trainers start out pricing their workshops at $25,000. But, once trainers get to the point where an event sells out extremely fast, they know it's time to start raising the price of admission. With fewer opportunities to see them live, followers of these trainers make a point of turning out for the more infrequent workshops. At some point, trainers are able to put on half of the workshops they used to and earn twice the money. This is how workshop prices rise to the five figure range.

Now, let's go to the opposite end of the spectrum to the companies charging $199 for their classes. This is by far as close as you're going to get to mass produced workshops. With a slew of trainers presenting the same workshop across the country every day, they need to be constructed in a way that accommodates the expertise levels of all of their presenters. This does not result in rich material, but it does result in a low price, which they no doubt make up for in volume.

Lastly, there are workshops that cost $2400, $1200, $797, $500 or $397 to attend. When someone considers attending a workshop they tend to entertain two questions, who are you, and how do I know your workshop will be worth my time and money? When considering a workshop taught by an unknown entity, the description of the workshop and the trainer's bio is often all one has to go on. When that's the case, the price tag tends to match the risk of the unknown, for example, $397 for a full-day workshop. As workshops grow in popularity, they can quickly jump up the price ladder. However, when a workshop doesn't draw a good crowd, trainers tend to keep the price low.

With that said, it's very important to resist the urge to charge too little for your workshops. A low-priced workshop sends the signal that you're either a nobody, or the workshop isn't that great.

It's better to charge too much than to charge too little. If you charge too much, you may not start off with a large turn out, but through delivery of a great workshop you demonstrate that you're worth the price. As word spreads, and as attendees provide you with testimonials you gain social proof that your workshops are, in fact, worth ones time and money, and you will be on your way to building a following at that price.

Take some time when pricing your workshops. Think in terms of your information and what it will mean to people, not in terms of affordability. Let's revisit the RFP workshop, as an example. If a business owner can learn how to win government contracts, it could mean hundreds of thousands of dollars to the company over the years. If you charge $250 for this material because you can't imagine anyone paying more, perhaps because you don't attend workshops above this price, you're sabotaging your efforts.

We expect value to be expressed through price; there's just no way around that. With that price you send the signal that your information couldn't possibly mean hundreds of thousands of dollars in contracts because it costs so little to access the information; it just doesn't compute. It's like a company trying to sell you a vacuum cleaner for $20 promising that it's superior to the $400 machine you currently own. They would have a far easier time convincing you that their $700 machine is superior, even if the two machines are identical. Likewise, when you under price your workshop that's on par with or superior to other workshops in the marketplace, you do yourself a disservice because your price tag sends a signal of inferiority.

So, think value, not affordability, when you price your workshops. Besides, if consumers only bought what they could afford, far fewer people would have the homes, cars, or vacation photos that they do, not to mention the shoes that line their closets. People find the money for the things in which they find value. Your role is simply to choose a topic that is of value and to assign a representative price to it. We will discuss audiences in a moment.

Trainer Precautions

Whether you hire a trainer or you use someone currently employed at the organization, protect your enterprise by not allowing trainers to get involved with the business side of things. Have your legal person draft a document that stipulates that workshop clients and referrals arising from workshops belong to the agency, and have your trainers sign it. Do not let your trainers negotiate the logistics of the training with the client or have access to their contact information. This information is valuable and needs to be kept confidential. Nor should trainers develop the relationship with those who hire you. Trainers need only know how their schedules are shaping up each month.

Why are these restrictions important? Because when companies want to put more of their people through a training they enjoyed in the past, they call the person they have the relationship with who made that training happen. If they dealt with Sally, they'll call Sally. If Sally ever decides to cut the organization out of the loop, it would be extremely easy for her to do so if she has those relationships and contact information.

Likewise, trainers should never pick up the check from the client. There is no need for trainers to even know how much the organization earns from the trainings. They get a paycheck, and that's all they should know when it comes to money. Many of the large national training organizations pay their traveling trainers $250 for the day, a $40 or $50 per diem, and a small commission from any product sales. Whatever you choose to pay your presenters, it will be a far cry from the thousands you'll be earning from behind the scenes. By simply taking a few precautions, you make it easier for everyone to behave ethically.

Logistics

When it comes to where you might hold a workshop, make it easy on yourself. If you're not being hired by a group to come in to train their people on their premises, hold your workshop in a low-cost or no-cost setting like your own conference room, if you have one. Alternatively, research places that allow nonprofits to use their facility at no cost, perhaps a library or university. Reach out to large companies, like your local public utility or phone company to see about free use of their conference room. They tend to have great rooms for meetings and trainings and they often extend them to the community. If you have no other choice but to use a hotel, contact the smaller ones in your area, and inquire about the days of the week that offer the best price. Also, make sure their cancellation policy is amenable to you.

Marketing to Strangers

When your stakeholders are a natural group for you to market your workshops to, you don't need to be very creative about marketing strategies, you just simply need to promote your workshops to your people. We will discuss this in the next section. In this section, we will discuss approaches for marketing outside of your sphere of influence.

Naturally, you'll have your webmaster add a page to your site for workshops that does a great job of marketing them to site visitors. If writing sales copy is not your forte, you can hire a writer at elance.com, or the like, to write your site's sales letter. Your page should include testimonials you've received from any paid or free presentations you've given over the years. If you've never asked for any, it's easy enough to ask for them now.

Have someone from your office attend the first workshop with you for the sole purpose of getting as many video testimonials as possible. If you have an iPad (4th generation or higher), or a simple digital recorder, like the Kodak Zi8 (under $100), you can take high quality recordings. The audio is good on the iPad up to about four feet away from your subject, and nothing compares to the simplicity of editing with the iMovie App. The Zi8 can take an external microphone, making it possible to get good sound, and it has a USB swing arm that pops out and plugs into your computer, which makes it easy to upload your video for editing.

Surveys

Surveys can help you identify, connect with, and market to potential workshop attendees, in addition to making it easy to zero in on topics that are important to them. As mentioned earlier, surveymonkey.com makes administering them very simple.

Let's say an organization that serves seniors has decided to offer workshops targeted at owners of home health care agencies. In preparation for sending the survey, the organization reaches out to these agencies with an email that introduces their services and which inquires about the services the agency provides. This initial outreach ensures the organization won't be spamming the agency when they send the survey.

A survey of this kind should be extremely brief, having no more than four questions. Its aim is simply to unearth some of the biggest challenges facing the business, agency, group, association, or organization. You promise to send them the results of the survey, which is useful information for them. Your returned surveys give you insights into how you can help this group, and you can use this information to design a workshop for them.

In the case of the organization marketing to home health care agencies, let's say they learned from the survey that these agencies are having a hard time obtaining payment for their services with recent changes in Medicare laws, and this organization is brilliant at this. Through this simple survey, the organization now has a topic for a workshop they might not otherwise have thought of, and they're already in conversation with their target audience. They put together a webinar for this group. When they send out the results of the survey, they send it with an invitation to attend the free webinar titled, *What the New Medicare Laws Mean for Home Health Care Agency Payments*. The organization knows for a fact that this is a webinar this group would be interested in attending, because it was generated from them. The next section will go into extensive detail about the format for webinars used to promote your workshops.

There is no reason for the organization to only send the results of the survey to those who participated in it. If they reached out to 100 agencies and only 30 completed the survey, they could still invite all 100 agencies to their promotional webinar. The survey results could help them with their future marketing as well. Moving forward, they would be able to utilize the replay of the Medicare webinar, simply getting on at the end to field questions.

Free Presentations

If you have been giving free presentations, you should inform these contacts of what you'll now be offering for a fee. Ask them for help spreading the word; after all, you've helped them with your time and information over the years. If you haven't been giving free presentations, you might want to consider becoming a luncheon speaker for your local clubs, such as Kiwanis, Rotary, Lyons, and the Chamber of Commerce, or any other organization in your area that needs speakers. Speaking for free should be done with the purpose of landing paid speaking or training opportunities, which is why it's important to be in front of the right group. If your workshops are for business owners, that's who you need to get in front of. If they're for individuals, go to associations or clubs that will get you in front of their people.

In your presentation, be sure to mention a couple of times something along the lines of, "When I train organizations on xyz, one of the questions I get asked a lot is. . ." or "one of the things I feel is key for them to grasp is. . ." This lets your audience know that you train on this topic.

Create a leave-behind piece that has your contact information on it, whether a presentation handout or a resource page of some kind. Resources on a page give attendees a reason to hold on to your material. You may want to put the title of the workshop you're currently promoting on it as well, or if you're not taking enrollments at the time, simply include something to the effect of, *Contact us for your xyz training needs.* You may want to offer a discount for club members, or anyone referred by a club member who attends your workshop within a certain timeframe.

Mini Workshop

The best way to approach this next marketing technique is to hire a few people to execute it. This strategy involves offering a free 20 minute mini training at the office of your target audience during one of their staff meetings. When calling to arrange this, inform the manager that at the end of your 20 minutes you will be extending an invitation to the group to attend a full session on the topic. If the topic is relevant and has value for the company's people, having you come in is a no-brainer.

What might this technique look like? An organization focused on the environment might create a half-day workshop for companies that install solar panels. They would have their presenters contact solar companies for this free 20 minute presentation. Since this organization's expertise is in green energy, they're going to educate the company's salespeople so that they're not solar peddlers, they're green consultants who are able to do a better job for their customers and close more business.

By providing a few gems during the 20 minutes it makes it clear what attendees could expect from a full workshop. At the conclusion of the training, presenters will ask the group if they found value in the topic, and they'll proceed to introduce your workshop, where attendees are guaranteed to receive more of the same valuable information. Presenters then describe what it will cover. After whetting everyone's appetite, they will hand out a registration form and go into the time, place, and the cost, and then very slowly they will go over the information needed to register: "All I need from you today is your name, your address, a telephone number, and your email so we can send you a confirmation, and as you can see I'm prepared to take MasterCard or Visa today, all you need to do is write your card number right there on the line provided, and don't forget to enter your expiration date."

By speaking slowly and deliberately while going through this section, it sends the signal that the form isn't meant to be tucked into a desk drawer, it's meant to be filled out today, right now, in fact. And then after a slight pause the presenter announces, "And for those of you taking action right now, that's right I can see you successful decisive types already filling in the form. For you action takers I want you to put a line through the $997 you see listed there, and replace it with $797." Presenters should then look at their watch and say, "Now, beside that price I want you to write tomorrow's date, 11/20/13, and the current time 9:45 a.m. That's exactly when this take action price expires, exactly 24 hours from now."

The deadline is important. The truth is that most of your enrollments will come from those who take action on the spot, with only a few trickles later. You could extend the deadline by a month and it would have no significant impact on enrollments. The only thing you risk by not imposing a deadline are the enrollments that come from the people who are ready to take action but who would procrastinate if given the chance. To avoid losing those people, you need a deadline. And, it's very important that the office staff enforce the deadline with any inquiries they may receive. After all, your presenters will return to that office.

That's the beauty of this technique, presenters can go back each year you have new material. Previous attendees will know it's a good workshop and will look forward to the refresher and to the new information. There may also be new-hires, not to mention those who weren't at the previous staff meeting and missed the presentation. And of course, there will be those who failed to enroll last time. In short, going back makes perfect sense. And, rest assured that if there is just one person in that room who paid the full price because of failing to meet the deadline they will practically do the presenter's job for them when the deadline is mentioned.

When it comes to hiring presenters there is no better interview than an audition. It's quite simple to hold a brief group interview that provides an overview of the work, making sure to inform candidates that they will be responsible for setting their own presentation appointments.

You would provide candidates with an audio recording of the 20 minute presentation as well as a transcript of it. Give them a couple of weeks to memorize it and return for the audition. On the day of the auditions, have each candidate stand in front of the room and present, with the other candidates serving as an audience. Stop them after you've seen enough to form an opinion, so that you can keep things moving. With a few presenters out there, it makes it very easy for you to always have packed workshops.

Referrals

It's always important to ask for referrals, but if your workshops are for a certain group of professionals that hire you to come in to train their people, you have a perfect opportunity to build a strong referral business. Getting referrals for workshops is one of the easiest things there is to do, and getting them should be taken very seriously. Here is one way to get referrals. Create a referral sheet that offers thank you gifts in exchange for referrals that become workshop clients.

One side or your referral page should display four gift items that have a high perceived value, yet which you can buy inexpensively from a place like B&F (bnfusa.com), as discussed earlier. Referrers can choose one of the four gifts for each successful referral. On the reverse side, create a place for four names and contact information, and put your fax number and email at the top of it.

Hand your referral forms out during your workshop—there's no better time or place to ask for referrals than right on the spot. However, don't make the mistake of handing them out at the end of your workshop. If it's a full-day event, hand them out right before you announce your break for lunch. Take a minute to explain the program thoroughly. Some people will fill out the form during lunch, others who arrive back to their seats early from lunch will fill it out then.

Before you take the last break of the day hold up the sheets you've collected, and briefly remind people of it again. At the end of the workshop, as you're concluding and thanking people for being such great participants, make one last request: "Referrals are the lifeblood of my organization's workshop series. If you valued what you learned today, the greatest thank you is with a referral, and we'll repay that kindness with a thank you gift of our own. If you don't want to supply us with your associate's contact information, that's fine, why not shoot them an email yourself, we always ask how people heard of us, so we'll be sure to credit you with the referral. Whatever works best—we greatly appreciate the support."

Don't be shy about asking for referrals, if you did a good job, providing a referral is simply a reciprocal act.

Marketing to Your People

If your people are your target audience for your workshops, half of your work is already done, the half where you must answer the question discussed earlier, who are you? Your existing relationship also provides you with a sense of the kind of workshop they would value. You could, of course, reach out to them with a survey to be sure you've dialed that in as closely as possible. With the subject matter in place, you simply need to invite them to your workshops. We will now discuss techniques for doing that.

A very effective way to invite your stakeholders and online following to a workshop is by offering a free webinar or teleseminar on the subject that serves as a preview. This will be a free class that will contain good content as well as a few commercials to promote your workshop. You tell the listeners what they need to do to be successful at the topic, you explain why they need to do it, as well as the importance of doing it, but you don't give all of the steps for how to do it. You do, however, discuss the importance of learning how to do it. And that makes for a good workshop preview webinar. And, just as a good movie preview makes you want to go see the movie, a good workshop preview makes you want to go to the workshop.

But, you need to strike a balance between content and commercial. You never want to make anyone feel as if your class was merely a sales pitch. You want to make your ratio of content to commercial 5 to 1 in favor of content. Timing is one of the most important things to get right here. A 75 minute presentation gives you enough time to educate and promote, and research has proven it to be an effective time length. However, people do tend to drop off at the 30 and 60 minute marks, so it's important to promote your workshop prior to these times.

You also want to give people a reason to stay on the call until the end. The goal is to give so much value that your attendees are hoping you have a home-study course they can buy, or a seminar they can attend. This enthusiasm is more likely to occur if they stay with you for the entire length of the class, which is why it's important to incentivize staying for the duration.

To do this you want to kick off the class by letting attendees know that as a thank you to those who stay on the teleseminar/webinar to the end you have a special gift: "The gift is valued at $47, but I'm giving it to you for free. The very fact that you're in attendance means you'll love this gift. But it's only for those who stay with me, it won't be available on the replay. So, be sure to stay with me because I'm going to tell you how to claim it later." What you don't want to do is tell them exactly when you'll be making the announcement, because people may leave and rejoin at that time.

At about 25 minutes into the class, before the 30 minute drop off mark, stop and acknowledge the value of what you've already shared, "So, those are the first two strategies I wanted to share with you. I have another killer strategy which I'll get to in a few minutes. Later in the class I'm going to tell you how to claim your $47 free gift. But, before I go on I want to ask you a question. There are 10 elements that proposals are scrutinized for, what do you suppose is the number one element, the one thing that if you get wrong nothing else matters? I'm going to share another great strategy with you in just a few minutes, but first I want you to think about the answer to this question, because when you're competing for thousands of dollars in contracts can you really afford not to know the answer to this question? On October 25th I'll be holding a workshop in San Francisco where I'll be explaining all 10 elements, including this most important one. You'll see examples of losing proposals. You'll discover the biggest mistake people are making when responding to RFPs. And, we'll look for each of the 10 elements in a winning proposal."

After you've described what the workshop will cover give them a call to action and an incentive to take that action: "As my way of rewarding decisive people, I have something special for the first 20 people who enroll in the workshop at the website shown here. The first 20 people are going to get a free 30 minute telephone consultation session with me, that can be utilized any time after the workshop to discuss any topic you choose. My normal consulting fee is $950 an hour, so this is a $475 bonus. The first 20 people who sign up will also receive a copy of the eBook *Failure is Not an Option*, and you will also receive a recording of a 45 minute interview with three representatives from the GSA. There are some real gems in this baby. So, hurry on over to the website so you can be sure to be one of the 20 who will receive these great bonuses."

On a webinar you would have a slide that lists your bonuses and your enrollment website page. You would also type the website into the chat box where it becomes a hyperlink that can be clicked on. Don't take more than five minutes for this commercial and then take them back into the material, "Okay are you ready for the killer strategy I promised? Let's get to it."

In another 25 minutes, which will be five minutes to the hour, another big drop off time, take another five to eight minutes to chime in again with, "Now, remember, I have something special for you that I know you'll appreciate, and I'm going to tell you how to claim that gift in a few minutes, but first I just have to say that I've decided to give you a bit more than I promised when you enrolled for this teleseminar/webinar. I'm going to give you a bonus strategy, and I'm going to give it to you in just a few minutes. But before I do I want to ask you, have you ever wondered why it seems like the same companies get awarded bid after bid? I can't wait to share this extra bonus strategy with you, but first I want to tell you a bit more about the unique opportunity to participate in my RFP workshop. You see, in my many years in this field I've learned why it is that some companies do, in fact, win contract after contract. The funny thing is that they're not necessarily bringing something better to the table than the next guy, but there is a reason for their success. In my workshop on October 25th in San Francisco, the beautiful city by the Bay, I'll be revealing strategies that these folks would probably prefer that I keep to myself."

After hitting some highlights, restate the call to action and then get back into the program, "Okay, let's get to the final bonus strategy, and the information for claiming your gift."

At the 70 minute mark you're saying something like, "Okay, thank you for joining me on this teleseminar/webinar. I trust you've benefited from the information, including the extra material. And, now please accept as my gift to you a free copy of the $47 eBook *Understanding RFPs Before you Rest in Peace: What No one Ever Tells You About Winning Contracts.* To claim your copy send an email to xyz@123.com, with 'Free Gift' in the subject line." Give one final pitch for the workshop and then close: "I hope you've enjoyed the call. I'm sure you'll agree that it was packed with valuable information that you can now use in your efforts to win awards. I also hope you'll join me in San Francisco." And disconnect.

A couple of notes here about the free gift. Clearly, you want to make your gift a digital download. You don't want to expend time or money shipping something you're giving away for free. You might have a few special reports that you can bring together cohesively into an eBook, or you may simply give away five special reports on the topic. If you're selling your reports for $10 each that's a $50 value. You can offer a recorded interview with an authority on a topic, or a recorded teleseminar. By simply reading some of your valued material into a microphone and recording it, you now have a downloadable Mp3 recording you can use as a gift.

Now, a quick note about bonuses. Bonuses are a great way to incentivize taking immediate action because procrastination can turn into no action. Tracking the first 20 people to enroll is simply a matter of counting the first 20 emails your shopping cart sends after an order is placed. If you prefer, you can be generous and provide the bonuses to everyone who enrolls that day, especially if the bonuses are simply digital products.

Consulting makes a great bonus. However, if you have no interest in providing a consultation then certainly don't offer it. But, you should know that although people feel like they've scored with a free consulting session, they rarely take advantage of it.

If the consulting time is redeemable after the workshop, attendees will probably already have most of their questions answered, which reduces the likelihood even further that it will be used. There's really no need to put an expiration date on the offer, because the more time that passes the less likely it becomes that it will be used, and it has more value to the recipient if it is open-ended.

There is actually a benefit to you if you do get a few requests for consulting. First, you might uncover a new workshop topic. And, second, you can create a new digital product from it. All you have to do, if you have recording software installed, is plug a microphone into your computer and put the mic near your mouth as you speak on the phone. Don't put the call on speakerphone; however, because you don't want to record the call, only your responses. At the end of the call you will have captured 30 minutes of yourself, basically, teaching on a topic.

You can either edit the recording, leaving you with a new Mp3 product, or you can have your answers transcribed, and after cleaning it up a bit, since the spoken word tends not to be acceptable written material as is, you now have a new special report or eBook.

Once you get a successful promotional webinar under your belt, meaning it resulted in a healthy 30 percent of attendees enrolling in your workshop, why should you hope that all the stars align for you the next time you're promoting the same workshop? You don't have to, you can simply use the replay. Just be careful not to accidentally put a date stamp on it with references to holidays, or the season, or major events like who's ahead in the World Series.

Special thanks to Tim Paulson for his research.

STRATEGY NUMBER 12: Monetize Services You Currently Offer For Free

To begin dissecting this strategy ask yourself, are we providing free services or products to an unintended group? For a good example of this point, let's revisit the organization mentioned earlier that helps individuals challenged by the condition lymphedema. One form of relief for this condition is a very special kind of lymphatic massage. Let's say this organization has always provided a free class to individuals with the condition and their family members, so they can learn how to perform this massage technique, but over time physical therapists, and occupational and massage therapists have started attending the free classes as well. Clearly, the organization's free services have spilled over to an unintended group, and it would make sense for them to correct this. Do you need to make a similar correction with some of your free services?

What about discounts, if you offer a discount to nonprofit organizations, is it a tiered rate? It's common for organizations with large budgets to be charged more than organizations with smaller budgets. Wouldn't a tiered rate make more fiscal sense for you as well, one that offers your current discount to the organizations with the smallest budgets, reducing the discount from there for larger organizations?

Another approach to this strategy is to consider programs you have in place that could be customized for private sector companies. For example, an organization might teach individuals who are disabled how to discuss their accommodation needs with employers. This same free material could be monetized if it were adjusted to address employers directly, helping them to ensure that they're ADA compliant.

This strategy could also entail charging for consulting services rather than giving all of your time away for free. You could even *pursue* consulting clients. If you are in a position to help a company better serve your people because you have first-hand knowledge about their needs, it would be a service to your people, as well as to the company, to consult with them. An organization that helps seniors, for example, might be aware of the challenges they have navigating the websites of certain companies that want their business. This is very valuable information that this organization could charge companies a telephone consulting fee to access.

And lastly, consider the material you use in your programs, not only could some of it perhaps be fleshed out to become a manual for businesses, or perhaps a certification program, but you may have the makings of a course that would satisfy continuing education units for certain professionals. Some of the online continuing education topics for social workers, for example, include aging and long-term care, HIV/AIDS, mental health, sexuality and sexual abuse, substance abuse, and veterans. Professionals with licensing requirements to satisfy are always looking for fresh interesting continuing education courses to take.

You never know what goldmine you're sitting on until you start thinking in terms of monetizing what you currently offer for free.

STRATEGY NUMBER 13: Promote Affiliate Products

Generating revenue through affiliate marketing involves promoting products and services that have your stamp of approval, complement your work, and benefit your people.

Although Amazon was one of the first companies to offer an affiliate program back in 1996, since that time many companies of all sizes have followed suit. You might be surprised to discover the companies that have an affiliate program these days.

Dollar Rent A Car Launches Web Site Affiliate Program, Members Earn Payment

Contact: Emily Gill
Dollar Rent A Car
918/669-2949
egill@dollar.com

TULSA, OKLA.- January 22, 2001: **Dollar Rent A Car**, winner of the Gomez Advisors Best Car Re

WeightWatchers

about us
join the weightwatchers.com affiliate program!

Companies offering affiliate programs

Basically, there are three ways to earn income through affiliate marketing. After signing up as an affiliate for a company, you're assigned a unique link to the company's website or to the product itself. Some companies will pay you a set amount for each visitor you send to their website, regardless of whether the visitor makes a purchase. This is known as *pay per click*. Some companies will pay you for the action taken once a person gets to the site, for example, if they register for something, or if they download something. This is known as *pay per lead.* And then there's the self-explanatory *pay per sale.*

It's easy enough to find out if a company has an affiliate program by simply doing an online search on the company name, followed by "affiliate program." For example, a search on the term *weight watchers affiliate program* will return the page shown above. When you're on a company's site you can look around, often at the bottom of the page, to see if you spot "affiliate opportunity."

You can also use an affiliate network to find programs. With so many companies offering affiliate programs, affiliate networks were formed to act as a third party middleman between merchants and affiliates. Networks are free for affiliates to join and they make it easy for you to find programs. They're put at your fingertips, they're categorized, and they're searchable. There are hundreds of networks, but you'll have access to plenty of merchants and literally millions of products by just joining, without any commitment, the major three: Linkshare, linkshare.com, Clickbank, clickbank.com, and Commission Junction, cj.com.

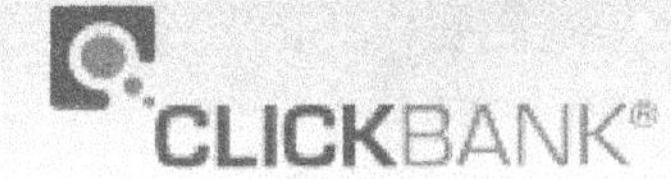

CLICKBANK®
Children Learning Reading
Super Effective Program Teaches Young Children To Read. 65% Commission. Video Sales Letter + Video Proof = Great Conversions. Steady 1.1% On All Traffic. Top Aff. Gets 1 In 20 Converts! For Aff Tools Go:
Http://www.childrenlearningreading.com/affiliates

Sample of an affiliate product offered at clickbank.com

To illustrate how an organization might incorporate affiliate marketing into the work they do, let's envision an organization that helps women establish credit in their name after exiting an abusive relationship. For years this organization has recommended CitiBank, Discover Card, and Bank One to their clients. Having signed up with Commission Junction, they did an "advertiser product search" on the words *credit cards* and discovered that all three credit card companies offer an affiliate program.

After signing up as an affiliate, or publisher as they're also called, with all three companies, they continue to recommend these credit cards as they've always done, but now when a client fills out a CitiBank application the organization earns $5, regardless of whether the applicant is approved or not. Discover and Bank One pay on approvals only. So, when someone uses the organization's affiliate link to visit Discover Card's site and they get approved for a card, the organization earns $25. And, when someone uses their affiliate link and gets approved for a Bank One card, the organization earns $50.

The organization also found an eBook at ClickBank on credit repair that pays $21 in commission. They purchased the book to make sure it had their stamp of approval. (Some affiliate programs allow you to make purchases through your own affiliate link, which equates to buying items at a discount, some programs forbid this.) They took the marketing material provided by the owner of the eBook and they used it to make a page for their site, utilizing their affiliate link. Now, every time a visitor to that page clicks on their affiliate link and buys the eBook the organization earns $21.

Hopefully, you're getting a sense of, if not some ideas for, how you might fold affiliate marketing into your organization's work. Affiliate marketing allows you to offer more to your people without having to create the product, or carry inventory, or handle order fulfillment.

A company's terms will define the structure of the affiliate relationship. Some programs allow you to make money from a visitor regardless of what they buy on the site, because that person used your affiliate link to visit the site. Some programs will pay a second tier of commission. As an example, let's say the client who bought the above organization's credit repair book liked it so much that he became an affiliate as well. A tiered commission program would pay the organization a small commission from his sales in addition to their own. Some companies, like Amazon, pay you for the one time a person visits the site and buys, while other companies pay you for two or three visits, or for a month or two, and still others pay for a lifetime. Some affiliate programs offer an opportunity to earn residual income, these involve a purchase that requires monthly payments to retain. With each monthly payment, you earn a commission.

Marketing Affiliate Products or Services

Hopefully you can already imagine how easy it would be to market affiliate products or services through your website and e-letter, and by utilizing the marketing techniques previously discussed. You may want to revisit the discussions for marketing eBooks, physical books, and media, because those techniques can be applied to affiliate products as well. You can also use affiliate products in conjunction with some of the other strategies introduced. For example, we discussed using an upsell to increase revenue generated from hosting webinars/teleseminars, this could easily be an affiliate digital product.

Without the need to buy or create anything, or even to write sales copy, in many cases, this is a strategy that should take no time at all to launch. If, however, you feel like you need more information on the topic, Rosalind Gardner, who's known as the Affiliate Marketing Queen because of the income she's earned promoting affiliate products, has written a 200 page eBook on the topic. You can purchase a copy at superaffiliatehandbook.com

STRATEGY NUMBER 14: Offer a Coaching Program

It has to be assumed that you have an expertise in your field that's valued or your organization probably wouldn't exist. There is quite possibly an aspect of that expertise that people would pay to be coached in.

Although coaching is feared by some to be time consuming, nothing could be further from the truth when the group session model is utilized. Group sessions, which are typically 60-80 minutes in length, are held once a month using the teleseminar or webinar companies discussed earlier. A recording of the call is provided members, either as a CD or an Mp3 download, depending on the cost of the coaching program. And, for webinars the replay is provided. That's it. There is no need to speak with coaching members outside of their coaching session.

If you assume an 80 minute monthly session, and add to that another two hours a month session preparation time, plus another two hours per month for marketing, and four hours a month for other matters related to coaching for good measure, we're looking at a 10 hour monthly investment of time. This is an incredible return on investment when you consider the monthly fees associated with coaching.

Below are the basic steps involved in launching this strategy, which will be discussed in detail on the pages to follow:

1. Research your best target audience.

2. Determine a monthly fee.

3. Name your program. Naming your coaching program is important. It helps to define it to prospective members, it simplifies your marketing, and it distinguishes it from the organization's other services.

4. Consider your content. This should be thought of in terms of quality not quantity. It's important not to overload members in an effort to ensure value in their eyes. A short weekly address by email, in addition to the monthly live session, is plenty of content. The goal should be to provide high quality relevant information that is results driven. Think more in terms of the therapist model rather than the professor. Unlike a professor, most therapists don't disseminate handouts or books. Clients pay therapists $300 a month or more not for the amount of material they can walk away with, but for the pertinent insights, encouragement, and action steps. So, likewise, think valuable, relevant, insightful, action-oriented, results driven sessions, not lots of curriculum, handouts, and homework.

5. Pull from the mailbag. Encourage coaching members to email questions to you for inclusion in the mailbag section of your weekly email address, where the question is answered. Such contact alerts you to the challenges facing certain members, challenges that other members may be able to relate to as well.

6. Mix things up. Occasionally invite members who've made recent strides to be a guest speaker. Interview authors, authorities on a topic, professors and trainers, as well as government representatives. Interviews are easier to get than you might think, yet they offer real value to your program.

Finding Your Target Audience

Successful coaching programs are those that help people with a vital part of their personal or professional life—improving finances, enhancing health, or bettering ones family life. Here are a few examples meant to get your creativity flowing. Let's take an organization in the arts. They would have a great deal to offer artists who have gained some recognition but who would like to take things to the next level. Being coached by an organization in the arts would offer an artist a great opportunity to achieve that. It would be wise for them to take applications and to restrict the artists they accept into the program to those who appear ready to achieve that next level. As word spreads, this could quite easily become a highly sought after coaching program.

As an organization with their finger on the pulse of the art community, they would be able to coach artists in what it takes to gain more exposure, to participate in a successful pop up gallery, and to get media attention, among other things. Clearly, this organization would have a lot to offer artists in a coaching program. However, they probably would be the last ones to see it.

You may be suffering from the same inability to see the people you could help. But you no doubt have your finger on the pulse of a community as well. Who could you help in a significant aspect of their lives from your insider's advantage? Maybe your coaching program will be designed around the professionals who serve your clients. As a referring agency you may think more in terms of the client side of the equation, but think about the professionals in business for themselves who account for the other side of the equation: the immigration lawyers, estate planners, credit counselors, long-term care professionals, home health care providers. Does your insider's understanding of their clients dictate what they could do to better serve, obtain, and retain clients? There just may be teachable information inside of those collective complaints you've heard over the years, information that could benefit a professional's career.

If just a few tips a month will help these professionals gain more clients, or acquire more referrals from happier clients, your coaching pays for itself. Take some time to do a brainstorming session, or perhaps create a mind map that involves listing people, or the professionals who help those people, who would benefit from your insights.

Marketing

When it comes to coaching, we prefer to be coached by people who we know, like, and trust. This means that the approach your marketing takes will depend on whether or not you already have a relationship with your target audience. When marketing to those with whom you already have a relationship, you simply need to introduce your program to them and give them a chance to apply or enroll. One way to do that is by inviting them to a free coaching webinar or teleseminar session, whichever format your group sessions will utilize. This session will provide a sense of what they can expect from the program. Naturally, you will record this promotional session so that you can use it going forward, only getting on at the end to field questions.

If, on the other hand, you're marketing to a group that doesn't know you, it's easier if you build that relationship first, thinking of coaching as the final wrung in the information delivery ladder. Your special reports, eBooks, webinars or teleseminars, and your workshops are a natural gateway to coaching.

So, again, build your list with an opt-in for a free digital product, and honor the integrity of your list by only offering products or services that align with the list's demonstrated interests. If someone has opted in to receive information on home schooling, for example, they shouldn't be included in the organization's mailings about breastfeeding simply because the organization educates on both topics. This is a quick way to reduce your list as quickly as you build it.

Conversely, if your actions demonstrate that your emails are relevant and worth reading you will have a high response rate when you mail to your list. Some of your mailings should strictly impart useful information while others will market a product or event. When it comes to the frequency of contact, it's important to strike the right balance between not being forgotten, and not becoming burdensome.

Some people on your list will demonstrate buying behavior in response to your emails, and they should be invited to your promotional coaching session. Let's think about it for a minute. If I downloaded your free special report *Five Steps to Writing Winning RFPs*, which included a description of a $47 eBook that I went on to buy, and later I invested in a couple of webinars on the topic, clearly I know like and trust you, which makes me a candidate for your coaching program.

It would be best to create a site devoted to your coaching program. Your main site should provide a link to the site, but it's important to have a site strictly dedicated to your coaching. One advantage this offers is that it will allow you to pick up online traffic from people searching on a topic that relates to your program. This is less likely to happen with your main site that offers disparate content. It also just makes for cleaner marketing.

Naming Your Program

Name your coaching program with an aim to making it easy to find and understand its purpose. Think in terms of the problem people might be typing into a search engine when naming your program. Use the Google keyword tool, mentioned earlier, to help you with this. If you name your coaching program with keywords in mind, and if you build a site dedicated to the topic, it's possible that your coaching site might come up in the search results when someone searches on the subject. This won't happen if you name the coaching program after your organization, or something obscure.

An organization that coaches businesses on how to win government contracts might be tempted to call their program the Veteran Alliance Coaching Program. But why would anyone type that into a search engine? However, according to Google, 4400 people are searching on the term "government contracts" every month. A program named *Government Contracts Coaching* would be the wiser choice of the two when it comes to hoping to be found online.

Pricing

As stated earlier, typical coaching fees run $97, 297, $497, $797, even $2,000 a month. Resist the urge to price yours below the norm, as lower priced programs are construed as lower in value. Carpet cleaners pay $10,000 a year to be a member of a coaching program hosted by Piranha Marketing, so don't pre-judge your audience.

The income potential for coaching can be significant. Even if you price your program in the lower middle of the spectrum at $247 a month, with as few as 50 members you'll earn over $12,000 a month, more than $148,000 a year. As previously stated, this is an incredible return on such a small investment of time of roughly 10 hours a month.

If you feel like you need assistance launching this strategy, visit the site of the head coach of coaching himself, Tim Paulson, at makemoneycoaching.com.

STRATEGY NUMBER 15: Offer Language Classes

The first element of this strategy involves doing a bit of research to determine what language(s) people in your community demonstrate an interest in learning. Which foreign languages have the most classes offered at your community college? What foreign language do you see the most posters for tutoring? Are there any groups listed in your area at meetup.com for people to practice a foreign language, if so which ones?

After you determine the language that would garner the most interest, the next step entails finding a part-time instructor equipped with their own curriculum. On the one hand, you shouldn't settle for the first person who raises their hand to say they speak the language, but you also don't need someone with a PhD in language studies. The best option is an experienced teacher who is fluent in the language, and who teaches in a compelling, fun, and effective manner. Your students will get totally caught up in the experience if it's compelling, they'll have a good time if it's fun, and their skills will improve if it's effective. That's the student retention trifecta. And, as a result, your classes will expand organically into an intermediate and an advanced level. A teacher with an extensive background in the language, but with a boring uninspiring teaching style is not going to get you these results. So, don't try to oversimplify things by using volunteers or someone at the agency simply because they speak the language.

Interviewing prospective instructors should consist of two phases. The first phase should involve having candidates come in with their curriculum to explain how they came about it and why, providing you with a chance to get a sense of their personality and such. Those who move on to the next phase will need to conduct a 20 minute class, where you, and perhaps staff, play the part of student. If you find the interviewee's teaching style to be compelling, fun, and effective it's fair to say that your students will too. These are the candidates you'll want to consider for the job.

Requiring a demonstration is extremely important. Anyone can sit in front of you and say their classes will hit the mark, but the one who can show you that in a mock lesson is the one that removes the need for faith. Let new hires know that student satisfaction is a strong basis for continuing, and create an instructor evaluation sheet so student's can provide you with feedback. Also, make a point of popping in on some of the first few classes yourself.

You will want to hire a few instructors for the part-time work. Although all of them may not be used initially, they will form a pool of instructors for you to choose from. This will also give you a reserve to draw from if an instructor calls in sick (set a strict policy for the amount of notice required for an absence). Having a pool of instructors will also allow you to ramp up quickly. You can start new classes and form intermediate and advanced classes as quickly as demand dictates.

These kinds of classes typically run an hour and a half. A small class size is a big draw for programs like this, and are best kept to eight, or 10 students at the most. Hopefully you can accommodate students in your conference room and keep expenses down.

Pricing

Private language classes typically run either six, eight, or 12 weeks. The following pricing structure is typical for classes that meet once a week: $220 for a six week class, $275 for an eight week class, and $360 for a 12 week class. An enrollment fee of $50 or $75 is common as well.

Now, you may not be able to appreciate why someone would pay $200 or $300 for a couple of months of language classes when they could just go up the street to the community college and pay so much less. However, one might also have a hard time understanding why someone would pay $80 to get their hair cut when there's a Super Cuts on the corner. In both cases, they serve different needs, and perhaps different clientele.

Instructor Compensation

Research what language tutors earn, and what the hourly rate is for a first year community college professor to determine fitting compensation for your instructors. Your registration fees should cover most, if not all, of your instructor's fees for an eight-week class. Let's say research leads you to pay your instructor $30 an hour. For a 1½ hour class, an instructor would earn $45, or $360 for an eight week class. The $400 generated from eight students paying a $50 registration fee takes care of your instructor's fees. This means the class tuition of, let's say, $275 is all yours. At that rate, ignoring the registration fee, with eight students in an eight week class, repeated six times a year you will net $13,200, two classes will net $26,400, three classes $39,600, and four classes will net over $52,800.

Marketing

Of course you'll have a website page for your classes, but being a local undertaking you'll want to do things like post flyers and have postcards printed that you can leave at retail establishments with a lot of foot traffic.

Send a PDF copy of your flyer to agencies and ask if they'll post it and forward a copy of it to their people or other agencies. Make sure your flyers and postcards consistently utilize the same color scheme so people will come to recognize you, even from across the room. If you have a weekly neighborhood paper that pulls well and that has reasonable ad rates you may want to advertise in it.

Keep doing whatever brings in students and discontinue what doesn't produce. This is why it's important to ask, and keep track of, how folks came to hear about the classes. Incentivize referrals from students by giving away an inexpensive but fun gift item for each referral that turns into a paid enrollment.

In addition to generating revenue, holding language classes will undoubtedly raise awareness about your organization. How could it not? What happens when students tell their friends that they're taking a language class? They will invariably ask where they're taking it, causing a conversation about your organization to ensue.

To see examples of this strategy, you may visit abclanguagesf.com, and casahispana.com.

STRATEGY NUMBER 16: Host a Membership Site

You may be wondering how a membership site would be any different from your organization's current site. The answer to this question defines membership sites. Whereas your main site is designed to serve the needs of all who visit it, a membership site is unapologetically devoted exclusively to one group. It's like belonging to an exclusive club. There's no need to wade through the cyber waste that riddles today's online ecosystem to get your needs met, because a membership site caters to those needs with consistently updated information. Who wouldn't appreciate having a well-organized place for fresh information on a subject of interest that they would otherwise have to go to Google, YouTube, and a news site to obtain. Additionally, it offers members a place for discussion, support, and, in some cases, friendship or camaraderie.

So, how might your organization utilize a membership site? Let's use the organization mentioned earlier that addresses the medical condition lymphedema for illustration purposes. While their main site might serve the needs of individuals who suffer from the condition, a membership site could serve the needs of medical professionals. It could provide the latest research in the field, and updates on treatment methodologies. Members could submit papers for the site. The site could provide case studies. A discussion forum, common to membership sites, would provide members with an outlet for posing questions and asking for feedback from colleagues on problem cases. Perhaps your stakeholders consist of two or more populations, one of whom you could customize a membership site for.

When thinking of a group, ask the same questions we pondered when considering workshop audiences, namely, who else serves your group? If you serve youth, what do their parents, teachers, counselors, career advisors, social workers, or foster parents need? What about the companies that employ your population?

Wouldn't employers who predominantly hire entry level workers and young employees, as well as career centers, benefit from membership to a site that provides training modules on work ethic, customer service, and conflict management that their people could utilize?

Content and Pricing

If your membership site is on the same subject as your digital products, you will be able to use this material for the site. Your special reports can be added to your site. That 50 page eBook can be dissected into 50 articles of 300-500 words each. Brochures can be turned into articles for your site members. In addition to articles, the site could provide video tutorials, video lectures, audio recordings, eBooks, a resource library, curated news content, or it might be an aggregator of information. Google Alerts, at google.com/alerts, is a very useful free tool for collecting content. It will send you an email that alerts you when news, blogs, videos, discussions, or books on your topic hit the web.

The replay or recording of any webinars or teleseminars you host can be posted on your membership site. It's quite simple to use screen capture software, like the earlier discussed Camtasia, to make a PowerPoint presentation out of some of your material to allow video to bring it to life.

The key is to launch the site with a wealth of information in place, and then once a week to add something new, keeping the site fresh. In exchange for this content, you will be able to generate revenue that is ongoing month after month and which continues to grow as new members join.

To see samples of sites and the fees that people are paying for their access, visit membergate.com, which will be discussed shortly, and click on *Clients*. You will see some sites that cost $99 to join and an additional $9.99 or $12.99 a month thereafter, while others offer tiered pricing, for example a $97, $147, $197,

$297 level for different degrees of access. And you will also find sites that simply charge $9.99, $15, or $29.95 a month.

Mechanics

So how do you put up a membership site? One of the easiest ways to create a membership site is with a company that allows you to build a site using their infrastructure, because a membership site has a lot of moving parts. For example, it needs to allow free browsing to some parts of the site for guests, but limit access to other parts. It needs to be able to determine when a person logs in whether their membership is current, and it then needs to allow or deny access accordingly. And, of course, the site offers recurring billing so that your member's credit cards get charged every month like clockwork without you lifting a finger.

With all of this going on you want software and an infrastructure designed to handle things seamlessly. People expect a site they're paying to access to be up and running flawlessly 24 hours a day. Membergate (membergate.com) is a leader in this field. Their license is by no means cheap at $3995, but the fee does include the designing of the site per your wishes, the security, functionality, and many features that make loading material to the site simple enough so as not to require any web design skills. They also offer a $197 a month option. This allows you to test the waters and build up your members, after which you can buy the license outright, saving you money in the long run.

The blogging and content management system, WordPress, has a plugin called Wishlist for creating membership sites that starts at $197 a month, but it doesn't come close to offering the same level of security as Membergate, and WordPress is notorious for getting hacked into. This is important to know because your webmaster will no doubt encourage you to go this route since so many designers use WordPress to build sites. However, with Membergate's $197 a month option, there is simply no reason to do so, especially if it's primarily to satisfy a webmaster's comfort zone.

Marketing your Membership Site

1. If you have a webmaster or search engine optimization professional who has helped you successfully drive traffic to your current site, request the same assistance for your membership site.

2. Utilize all appropriate marketing techniques discussed throughout the book for promoting your site.

3. Create a social networking campaign around the launch of the site.

4. Do a big email blast that announces its launch. Promote it in your e-letter, end of year letter, and any other appropriate marketing pieces you distribute.

5. Offer a $1 one month trial, with the understanding that the following month the regular membership fee will be charged automatically, unless they cancel. You don't want to offer a *free* trial because then you have to go back and ask for credit card information to bill them the following month.

6. Use a membership trial as an upsell for your webinars or teleseminars, as discussed in that section.

7. Have a membership site launch party, where the idea is to celebrate the site launch but also to enroll guests in the $1 trial membership. Have a table set up where credit cards can be swiped. Offer small but fun bonus gifts for enrollments. These can come from sponsors or from one of your bonus gift partners discussed in marketing your books. Post in a prominent place the number of

enrollments you want to achieve that night alongside the actual number and continue to update the number throughout the night. Get the crowd involved in helping you reach your goal.

8. Submit a public service announcement to the appropriate outlets.

9. Have brochures made that do an excellent job of describing the site and its contents and distribute them widely.

10. Hold a contest for volunteers that rewards everyone who reaches a specific number of $1 trial enrollments with a coveted prize. Whether they stand in a public area with a clipboard and brochures and enroll passersby, or they connect with their social networking community, encourage volunteers to get creative.

Why not decide from the outset the revenue you would like to see generated from your membership site, and determine the number of members required to meet that goal, then go about doing whatever it takes to hit that number. Never stop marketing your site in one way or another, so that despite drop offs you will be able to watch it expand exponentially over the years.

Strategic Financing

It's time now to discuss strategic financing for those strategies that might require some financial assistance to launch.

It's no secret that triangles are used in construction because of their inherent strength. A triangle also offers strength when it comes to funding. To introduce the strategic financing triangle, let's take a look at an organization that requires no introduction—Habitat For Humanity. How have they managed to build more than 200,000 homes in nearly 100 countries? Here's how: (1) they use volunteer labor; (2) they use donated materials; and (3) they require that homeowners pay a no-interest mortgage, which creates revenue for the local Habitat affiliate and is reinvested into building more homes. That is the strategic financing triangle in action: volunteer labor, in-kind donations, and a revenue generator.

San Francisco Bay Bridge
photo by Steven Damron

Some organizations miss a leg or two of this triangle. Maybe they're good at rallying volunteers, but they're not so good at getting in-kind donations, causing them to drain their resources.

Or, maybe they tend to employ both of these elements, but then they fail to install a revenue generator, which prevents the project from being sustainable. As demonstrated by Habitat, true long-lasting success requires an intact triangle.

Hosting a contest definitely requires a strategic financing triangle. As discussed at the outset, volunteers can be used as judges and for help with advertising, the entry fee is the revenue generator, and the prizes will be obtained through in-kind donations. It would be unwise to host a contest without employing an intact triangle.

Sponsorships

Being able to create partnerships and obtain sponsorships is another facet of strategic financing. Hopefully, you're already skilled at developing local partners and you have a few. This section is meant to get you thinking about building large corporate partnerships. Whether for help implementing strategies we've discussed here or for other projects, if you work with partners you should never have a problem financing your undertakings.

Never forget that you are the liaison between the community and corporations. You wear the white hat and carry the goodwill, while corporations often have to play defense when it comes to company image. Corporations are constantly in search of opportunities that allow them to either change an image, for example, banks may be in need of an image makeover after a financial crisis, or reinforce an image in the marketplace.

The simplest way to find sponsors is to find the corporations whose mission, market, and strategic goals align in some way with your mission, people, and projects. By simply spending some time at their website, you will learn of a corporation's mission. By reading their annual reports and press releases, linked to from their site, you will discover their strategic goals for the year. Once you know what a corporation is trying to do, and who they're trying to reach, you should be able to determine if you have the makings of a relationship. Once you've determined that this is the case, you would reach out to someone in the company's sponsorship department, this is often the VP of community development or outreach or social responsibility.

Working with partners in this way will allow you to launch some of the strategies we've discussed with fanfare. You might want to have an event that draws community and media attention to the launch of your membership site, as just discussed, or your first annual contest, or you may want to throw a screening party for your DVD. To do this you simply need to find a corporation aligned with your mission and people, and offer them a chance to partner with you on the event.

Using the launch of a membership site as an example, you might pitch a sponsor on a collaboration in this way: "Our organization reaches X thousand women annually as we provide them with ABC. Our membership site is going to be one more vehicle we will utilize to reach and serve the needs of these women who have come to rely on us for ABC. The site will be unique to their needs, and we are expecting it to be wildly successful based on the testing we've done. Since we know that you care about the needs of women too, we thought we'd come to you to see if there's an interest in sponsoring our site's launch. We've been playing around with some ideas about how we can launch with style, but we are eager to see what we could jointly create that would suit everyone's needs."

Now how much money might you ask for? Although the corporation doesn't need or even want you to itemize or break down the numbers as if you were pursuing a grant, we'll do it now for the sake of coming up with a number. As we know, the cost for a license at Membergate is $4,000. Let's say you pay someone another $1500 to produce all of your initial information products for the site, we're now up to $5,500. You decide a launch party would be a great way to create buzz around the membership site, and it would give your corporate sponsor something to sink their teeth into. The party brings your total to $20,000. You now have a number. What else might you want besides money? You may also want your sponsor to provide a link from their site to your membership site after it's up, for a duration of their choosing. Some corporations get a million visitors a month to their site.

Now that you know what you want from them, the next thing to think about is what are you going to give them in return? Bear in mind that you're certainly not trying to give them a dollar for dollar return on their money. It's more about considering the unique experience you can provide them. You could perhaps include them in your ad campaign: "The Women's Organization, in partnership with FedEx, announces the launch of their new membership site. . . ." Although an ad campaign might otherwise be cost prohibitive, with your sponsor's support it becomes possible. When considering what you can do for your partners, you should always think post-financing.

Additionally, at the launch party they would of course be listed on the program, as well as on any signage. You would also thank them from the stage throughout the night, and one of their representatives would probably speak. This is what you can offer, and, of course, they will have ideas of their own as you work together collaboratively.

Once you start thinking in terms of working with partners for your large undertakings, everything opens up and becomes possible. Once you start insulating programs with the strategic financing triangle you can feel confident in their sustainability.

Implementation

Well, there you have it, access to 16 strategies for monetizing your mission—strategies that are feasible, doable, and relatively painless, while promising a substantial no-strings attached income stream. Strategies that raise funds without fundraising. You've also been provided with marketing techniques for launching each strategy, as well as a look at strategic financing and partnerships. There's only one thing left to do and that is to take action.

So, with that I ask, how do you typically make sure a good idea doesn't either get put on a shelf or get ignored, or is that what tends to happen? We know that for an organization to continue to be successful it has to continue to be innovative, which by definition means having a willingness and capacity to implement new ideas. Do you have both of those? Investing in this book demonstrates a willingness to entertain new approaches to old problems. Now, you just need to take the next step and implement what you've learned.

This section will draw on the thinking of Peter Drucker, who it's been said of, "invented management." Having written material that's been deemed management literature classics, his opinion on the need for managers to take action deserves attention. Here are his thoughts on the subject:

1. It falls on the shoulder of executives to be forward looking, to continue to ask the question, "how can we do better what we're already doing?" Because, this is the question that promotes organizational health. Conversely, always searching for money prevents forward thinking.

2. Don't get stuck in the thinking of "this is how we've always done it, so let's just improve it a little bit." Executives need to know when to say, "Enough already. Let's stop improving and patching up the old rather than going all out for the new."

3. As you approach new ideas, don't start out with what you know, start out with what you need to learn. "Don't go

into an innovative idea saying, 'this is how we do it,' say instead, 'let's find out what this needs.' "

4. Don't buy into what everybody knows. "Well, everybody knows this didn't work last time we tried this approach. You know why you shouldn't buy into what everybody knows? Because what everybody knows is usually 20 years out of date."

Don't let what you've learned go to waste, sit on a shelf, or just get ignored. Don't let it get dismissed with antiquated thinking. You chose *now* to invest in this material, there's something to be said for that. Doesn't it make sense to also choose *now* to select a strategy and take it out for a spin?

Use the implementation planner on the pages to follow to help you move forward with these strategies. And, keep moving forward until you launch a strategy. Keep launching strategies until you reach a point where you never have to worry about where your next funding is coming from. That is going to be an amazing day, be sure to celebrate it.

—*I wish you nothing but the best and tons of success.*

STRATEGY IMPLEMENTATION PLAN	Page 1 of 3

Strategy: ____

Steps For Launching Strategy:
(Briefly list the most immediate steps for launching this strategy.)

1.

2.

3.

4.

Details:
(Provide the details for each corresponding number above.)

1.

2.

3.

4.

STRATEGY IMPLEMENTATION PLAN Page 2 of 3

Potential Resistance

(List the fear or lack of know-how or other resistance you foresee. List in order of highest concern.)

1.

2.

3.

4.

Plan for Overcoming Resistance

(List your plan for not being controlled by fear or lack of know-how for each corresponding item listed above.)

1.

2.

3.

4.

STRATEGY IMPLEMENTATION PLAN Page 3 of 3

Date for Launching Strategy: ______________________

Action Plan For Next Week

1.

2.

3.

4.

Actions Taken Last Week

1.

2.

3.

4.

Sample

Strategy: Write a Special Report.

Steps For Launching Strategy:
(Briefly list the most immediate steps for launching this strategy.)

1. Make a list of frequently asked questions.

2. Ask staff to compile their own list of frequently asked questions.

3. Cull the lists.

4. Write a special report in answer to one of the questions.

Details:
(Provide the details for each corresponding number above.)

1. Pull questions from old emails, look through logs.

2. Have Margaret and maybe Sheryl do the same thing and brainstorm other ways of gathering questions. Have them keep a log for a while.

3. Have Sheryl comb through the lists highlighting the ones that repeat and make me a master list.

4. Set aside time to write.

Potential Resistance

(List the fear or lack of know-how or other resistance you foresee. List in order of highest concern.)

1. I don't know if I'm going to have time for this.

2. I've never turned a document into a PDF.

3.

4.

Plan for Overcoming Resistance

(List your plan for not being controlled by fear or lack of know-how for each corresponding item above.)

1. Use the 30 minutes before staff arrives in the morning as quiet writing time. Have Margaret take messages off of the voicemail rather than doing it before she gets in, this will give me another 20 minutes for a total of 50 extra minutes a day for writing.

2. I don't have to know that right now. It's the last step in the process. I'm sure someone can help me with that.

3.

4.

Date for Launching Strategy: <u>5/11/13</u>

Action Plan For Next Week

1. Talk to Margaret and Sheryl about what I need.

2. Start working on my own list of frequently asked questions.

3. Narrow down the list to the five most frequently asked questions.

4.

Actions Taken Last Week

1. N/A

2.

3.

4.

INDEX

ABOUT THE AUTHOR

Award winning trainer and best-selling author, PAM HOGAN, holds a bachelor's degree in psycho-social theory from UC Berkeley, a master's degree in non-profit administration from the University of San Francisco, and a master's degree in criminal justice from Boston University.

Ms. Hogan began customizing trainings for public sector managers in 1994. She went on to found Pam Hogan Productions, a training and development company committed to helping the social and public sector better serve prisoners, veterans, marginalized and at-risk groups. Her training materials are requested by organizations from around the world.

www.ingramcontent.com/pod-product-compliance
Lightning Source LLC
Chambersburg PA
CBHW061741270326
41928CB00011B/2323

* 9 7 8 0 9 7 9 4 2 9 4 8 4 *